TO KILL A MOCKINGBIRD

Harper Lee

SPARK PUBLISHING

SPARKNOTES is a registered trademark of SparkNotes LLC

Spark Publishing
A Division of Barnes & Noble
120 Fifth Avenue
New York, NY 10011
www.sparknotes.com

ISBN-13: 978-1-4114-0515-8
ISBN-10: 1-4114-0515-3

Please submit changes or report errors to www.sparknotes.com/errors.

Printed in the United States.

10 9 8 7 6 5 4 3 2

Contents

CONTEXT

NELLE HARPER LEE WAS BORN on April 28, 1926, in Monroeville, Alabama, a sleepy small town similar in many ways to Maycomb, the setting of *To Kill a Mockingbird*. Like Atticus Finch, the father of Scout, the narrator and protagonist of *To Kill a Mockingbird*, Lee's father was a lawyer. Among Lee's childhood friends was the future novelist and essayist Truman Capote, from whom she drew inspiration for the character Dill. These personal details notwithstanding, Lee maintains that *To Kill a Mockingbird* was intended to portray not her own childhood home but rather a nonspecific Southern town. "People are people anywhere you put them," she declared in a 1961 interview.

Yet the book's setting and characters are not the only aspects of the story shaped by events that occurred during Lee's childhood. In 1931, when Lee was five, nine young black men were accused of raping two white women near Scottsboro, Alabama. After a series of lengthy, highly publicized, and often bitter trials, five of the nine men were sentenced to long prison terms. Many prominent lawyers and other American citizens saw the sentences as spurious and motivated only by racial prejudice. It was also suspected that the women who had accused the men were lying, and in appeal after appeal, their claims became more dubious. There can be little doubt that the Scottsboro Case, as the trials of the nine men came to be called, served as a seed for the trial that stands at the heart of Lee's novel.

Lee began *To Kill a Mockingbird* in the mid-1950s, after moving to New York to become a writer. She completed the novel in 1957 and published it, with revisions, in 1960, just before the peak of the American civil rights movement.

Critical response to *To Kill a Mockingbird* was mixed: a number of critics found the narrative voice of a nine-year-old girl unconvincing and called the novel overly moralistic. Nevertheless, in the racially charged atmosphere of the early 1960s, the book became an enormous popular success, winning the Pulitzer Prize in 1961 and selling over fifteen million copies. Two years after the book's publication, an Academy Award–winning film version of the novel, starring Gregory Peck as Atticus Finch, was produced. Meanwhile, the author herself had retreated from the public eye: she avoided interviews, declined to write the screenplay for the film version, and published only a few short pieces after 1961. *To Kill a Mockingbird* remains her sole published novel. Lee eventually returned to Monroeville and continues to live there.

In 1993, Lee penned a brief foreword to her book. In it she asks that future editions of *To Kill a Mockingbird* be spared critical introductions. "*Mockingbird*," she writes, "still says what it has to say; it has managed to survive the years without preamble." The book remains a staple of high school and college reading lists, beloved by millions of readers worldwide for its appealing depiction of childhood innocence, its scathing moral condemnation of racial prejudice, and its affirmation that human goodness can withstand the assault of evil.

PLOT OVERVIEW

SCOUT FINCH LIVES WITH her brother, Jem, and their widowed father, Atticus, in the sleepy Alabama town of Maycomb. Maycomb is suffering through the Great Depression, but Atticus is a prominent lawyer and the Finch family is reasonably well off in comparison to the rest of society. One summer, Jem and Scout befriend a boy named Dill, who has come to live in their neighborhood for the summer, and the trio acts out stories together. Eventually, Dill becomes fascinated with the spooky house on their street called the Radley Place. The house is owned by Mr. Nathan Radley, whose brother, Arthur (nick-named Boo), has lived there for years without venturing outside.

Scout goes to school for the first time that fall and detests it. She and Jem find gifts apparently left for them in a knothole of a tree on the Radley property. Dill returns the following summer, and he, Scout, and Jem begin to act out the story of Boo Radley. Atticus puts a stop to their antics, urging the children to try to see life from another person's perspective before making judgments. But, on Dill's last night in Maycomb for the summer, the three sneak onto the Radley property, where Nathan Radley shoots at them. Jem loses his pants in the ensuing escape. When he returns for them, he finds them mended and hung over the fence. The next winter, Jem and Scout find more presents in the tree, presumably left by the mysterious Boo. Nathan Radley eventually plugs the knothole with cement. Shortly thereafter, a fire breaks out in another neighbor's house, and during the fire someone slips a blanket on Scout's shoulders as she watches the blaze. Convinced that Boo did it, Jem tells Atticus about the mended pants and the presents.

To the consternation of Maycomb's racist white community, Atticus agrees to defend a black man named Tom Robinson, who has been accused of raping a white woman. Because of Atticus's decision, Jem and Scout are subjected to abuse from other children, even when they celebrate Christmas at the family compound on Finch's Landing. Calpurnia, the Finches' black cook, takes them to the local black church, where the warm and close-knit community largely embraces the children.

Atticus's sister, Alexandra, comes to live with the Finches the next summer. Dill, who is supposed to live with his "new father" in another town, runs away and comes to Maycomb. Tom Robinson's trial begins, and when the accused man is placed in the local jail, a mob gathers to lynch him. Atticus faces the mob down the night before the trial. Jem and Scout, who have sneaked out of the house, soon join him. Scout recognizes one of the men, and her polite questioning about his son shames him into dispersing the mob.

At the trial itself, the children sit in the "colored balcony" with the town's black citizens. Atticus provides clear evidence that the accusers, Mayella Ewell and her father, Bob, are lying: in fact, Mayella propositioned Tom Robinson, was caught by her father, and then accused Tom of rape to cover her shame and guilt. Atticus provides impressive evidence that the marks on Mayella's face are from wounds that her father inflicted; upon discovering her with Tom, he called her a whore and beat her. Yet, despite the significant evidence pointing to Tom's innocence, the all-white jury convicts him. The innocent Tom later tries to escape from prison and is shot to death. In the aftermath of the trial, Jem's faith in justice is badly shaken, and he lapses into despondency and doubt.

Despite the verdict, Bob Ewell feels that Atticus and the judge have made a fool out of him, and he vows revenge. He menaces Tom Robinson's widow, tries to break into the judge's house, and finally attacks Jem and Scout as they walk home from a Halloween party. Boo Radley intervenes, however, saving the children and stabbing Ewell fatally during the struggle. Boo carries the wounded Jem back to Atticus's house, where the sheriff, in order to protect Boo, insists that Ewell tripped over a tree root and fell on his own knife. After sitting with Scout for a while, Boo disappears once more into the Radley house.

Later, Scout feels as though she can finally imagine what life is like for Boo. He has become a human being to her at last. With this realization, Scout embraces her father's advice to practice sympathy and understanding and demonstrates that her experiences with hatred and prejudice will not sully her faith in human goodness.

CHARACTER LIST

Jean Louise "Scout" Finch The narrator and protagonist of the story. Scout lives with her father, Atticus, her brother, Jem, and their black cook, Calpurnia, in Maycomb. She is intelligent and, by the standards of her time and place, a tomboy. Scout has a combative streak and a basic faith in the goodness of the people in her community. As the novel progresses, this faith is tested by the hatred and prejudice that emerge during Tom Robinson's trial. Scout eventually develops a more grown-up perspective that enables her to appreciate human goodness without ignoring human evil.

Atticus Finch Scout and Jem's father, a lawyer in Maycomb descended from an old local family. A widower with a dry sense of humor, Atticus has instilled in his children his strong sense of morality and justice. He is one of the few residents of Maycomb committed to racial equality. When he agrees to defend Tom Robinson, a black man charged with raping a white woman, he exposes himself and his family to the anger of the white community. With his strongly held convictions, wisdom, and empathy, Atticus functions as the novel's moral backbone.

Jeremy Atticus "Jem" Finch Scout's brother and constant playmate at the beginning of the story. Jem is something of a typical American boy, refusing to back down from dares and fantasizing about playing football. Four years older than Scout, he gradually separates himself from her games, but he remains her close companion and protector throughout the novel. Jem moves into adolescence during the story, and his ideals are shaken badly by the evil and injustice that he perceives during the trial of Tom Robinson.

Arthur "Boo" Radley A recluse who never sets foot outside his house, Boo dominates the imaginations of Jem, Scout, and Dill. He is a powerful symbol of goodness swathed in an initial shroud of creepiness, leaving little presents for Scout and Jem and emerging at an opportune moment to save the children. An intelligent child emotionally damaged by his cruel father, Boo provides an example of the threat that evil poses to innocence and goodness. He is one of the novel's "mockingbirds," a good person injured by the evil of mankind.

Bob Ewell A drunken, mostly unemployed member of Maycomb's poorest family. In his knowingly wrongful accusation that Tom Robinson raped his daughter, Ewell represents the dark side of the South: ignorance, poverty, squalor, and hate-filled racial prejudice.

Charles Baker "Dill" Harris Jem and Scout's summer neighbor and friend. Dill is a diminutive, confident boy with an active imagination. He becomes fascinated with Boo Radley and represents the perspective of childhood innocence throughout the novel.

Miss Maudie Atkinson The Finches' neighbor, a sharp-tongued widow, and an old friend of the family. Miss Maudie is almost the same age as Atticus's younger brother, Jack. She shares Atticus's passion for justice and is the children's best friend among Maycomb's adults.

Calpurnia The Finches' black cook. Calpurnia is a stern disciplinarian and the children's bridge between the white world and her own black community.

Aunt Alexandra Atticus's sister, a strong-willed woman with a fierce devotion to her family. Alexandra is the perfect Southern lady, and her commitment to propriety and tradition often leads her to clash with Scout.

Mayella Ewell Bob Ewell's abused, lonely, unhappy daughter. Though one can pity Mayella because of her overbearing father, one cannot pardon her for her shameful indictment of Tom Robinson.

Tom Robinson The black field hand accused of rape. Tom is one of the novel's "mockingbirds," an important symbol of innocence destroyed by evil.

Link Deas Tom Robinson's employer. In his willingness to look past race and praise the integrity of Tom's character, Deas epitomizes the opposite of prejudice.

Mrs. Henry Lafayette Dubose An elderly, ill-tempered, racist woman who lives near the Finches. Although Jem believes that Mrs. Dubose is a thoroughly bad woman, Atticus admires her for the courage with which she battles her morphine addiction.

Nathan Radley Boo Radley's older brother. Scout thinks that Nathan is similar to the deceased Mr. Radley, Boo and Nathan's father. Nathan cruelly cuts off an important element of Boo's relationship with Jem and Scout when he plugs up the knothole in which Boo leaves presents for the children.

Heck Tate The sheriff of Maycomb and a major witness at Tom Robinson's trial. Heck is a decent man who tries to protect the innocent from danger.

Mr. Underwood The publisher of Maycomb's newspaper. Mr. Underwood respects Atticus and proves his ally.

Mr. Dolphus Raymond A wealthy white man who lives with his black mistress and mulatto children. Raymond pretends to be a drunk so that the citizens of Maycomb will have an explanation for his behavior. In reality, he is simply jaded by the hypocrisy of white society and prefers living among blacks.

CHARACTER LIST

Mr. Walter Cunningham A poor farmer and part of the mob that seeks to lynch Tom Robinson at the jail. Mr. Cunningham displays his human goodness when Scout's politeness compels him to disperse the men at the jail.

Walter Cunningham Son of Mr. Cunningham and classmate of Scout. Walter cannot afford lunch one day at school and accidentally gets Scout in trouble.

ANALYSIS OF MAJOR CHARACTERS

SCOUT

Scout is a very unusual little girl, both in her own qualities and in her social position. She is unusually intelligent (she learns to read before beginning school), unusually confident (she fights boys without fear), unusually thoughtful (she worries about the essential goodness and evil of mankind), and unusually good (she always acts with the best intentions). In terms of her social identity, she is unusual for being a tomboy in the prim and proper Southern world of Maycomb.

One quickly realizes when reading *To Kill a Mockingbird* that Scout is who she is because of the way Atticus has raised her. He has nurtured her mind, conscience, and individuality without bogging her down in fussy social hypocrisies and notions of propriety. While most girls in Scout's position would be wearing dresses and learning manners, Scout, thanks to Atticus's hands-off parenting style, wears overalls and learns to climb trees with Jem and Dill. She does not always grasp social niceties (she tells her teacher that one of her fellow students is too poor to pay her back for lunch), and human behavior often baffles her (as when one of her teachers criticizes Hitler's prejudice against Jews while indulging in her own prejudice against blacks), but Atticus's protection of Scout from hypocrisy and social pressure has rendered her open, forthright, and well meaning.

At the beginning of the novel, Scout is an innocent, good-hearted five-year-old child who has no experience with the evils of the world. As the novel progresses, Scout has her first contact with evil in the form of racial prejudice, and the basic development of her character is governed by the question of whether she will emerge from that contact with her conscience and optimism intact or whether she will be bruised, hurt, or destroyed like Boo Radley and Tom Robinson. Thanks to Atticus's wisdom, Scout learns that though humanity has a great capacity for evil, it also has a great capacity for good, and that the evil can often be mitigated if one approaches others with an outlook of sympathy and understanding. Scout's development

into a person capable of assuming that outlook marks the culmination of the novel and indicates that, whatever evil she encounters,
she will retain her conscience without becoming cynical or jaded.
Though she is still a child at the end of the book, Scout's perspective
on life develops from that of an innocent child into that of a near
grown-up.

ATTICUS

As one of the most prominent citizens in Maycomb during the Great
Depression, Atticus is relatively well off in a time of widespread
poverty. Because of his penetrating intelligence, calm wisdom, and
exemplary behavior, Atticus is respected by everyone, including
the very poor. He functions as the moral backbone of Maycomb,
a person to whom others turn in times of doubt and trouble. But
the conscience that makes him so admirable ultimately causes his
falling out with the people of Maycomb. Unable to abide the town's
comfortable ingrained racial prejudice, he agrees to defend Tom
Robinson, a black man. Atticus's action makes him the object of
scorn in Maycomb, but he is simply too impressive a figure to be
scorned for long. After the trial, he seems destined to be held in the
same high regard as before.

Atticus practices the ethic of sympathy and understanding that
he preaches to Scout and Jem and never holds a grudge against the
people of Maycomb. Despite their callous indifference to racial
inequality, Atticus sees much to admire in them. He recognizes that
people have both good and bad qualities, and he is determined to
admire the good while understanding and forgiving the bad. Atticus
passes this great moral lesson on to Scout—this perspective protects
the innocent from being destroyed by contact with evil.

Ironically, though Atticus is a heroic figure in the novel and a
respected man in Maycomb, neither Jem nor Scout consciously idol-
izes him at the beginning of the novel. Both are embarrassed that
he is older than other fathers and that he doesn't hunt or fish. But
Atticus's wise parenting, which he sums up in Chapter 30 by saying, "Before Jem looks at anyone else he looks at me, and I've tried
to live so I can look squarely back at him," ultimately wins their
respect. By the end of the novel, Jem, in particular, is fiercely devoted
to Atticus (Scout, still a little girl, loves him uncritically). Though
his children's attitude toward him evolves, Atticus is characterized
throughout the book by his absolute consistency. He stands rigidly

committed to justice and thoughtfully willing to view matters from the perspectives of others. He does not develop in the novel but retains these qualities in equal measure, making him the novel's moral guide and voice of conscience.

JEM

If Scout is an innocent girl who is exposed to evil at an early age and forced to develop an adult moral outlook, Jem finds himself in an even more turbulent situation. His shattering experience at Tom Robinson's trial occurs just as he is entering puberty, a time when life is complicated and traumatic enough. His disillusionment upon seeing that justice does not always prevail leaves him vulnerable and confused at a critical, formative point in his life. Nevertheless, he admirably upholds the commitment to justice that Atticus instilled in him and maintains it with deep conviction throughout the novel.

Unlike the jaded Mr. Raymond, Jem is not without hope: Atticus tells Scout that Jem simply needs time to process what he has learned. The strong presence of Atticus in Jem's life seems to promise that he will recover his equilibrium. Later in his life, Jem is able to see that Boo Radley's unexpected aid indicates there is good in people. Even before the end of the novel, Jem shows signs of having learned a positive lesson from the trial; for instance, at the beginning of Chapter 25, he refuses to allow Scout to squash a roly-poly bug because it has done nothing to harm her. After seeing the unfair destruction of Tom Robinson, Jem now wants to protect the fragile and harmless.

The idea that Jem resolves his cynicism and moves toward a happier life is supported by the beginning of the novel, in which a grown-up Scout remembers talking to Jem about the events that make up the novel's plot. Scout says that Jem pinpointed the children's initial interest in Boo Radley at the beginning of the story, strongly implying that he understood what Boo represented to them and, like Scout, managed to shed his innocence without losing his hope.

THEMES, MOTIFS & SYMBOLS

THEMES

Themes are the fundamental and often universal ideas explored in a literary work.

THE COEXISTENCE OF GOOD AND EVIL

The most important theme of *To Kill a Mockingbird* is the book's exploration of the moral nature of human beings—that is, whether people are essentially good or essentially evil. The novel approaches this question by dramatizing Scout and Jem's transition from a perspective of childhood innocence, in which they assume that people are good because they have never seen evil, to a more adult perspective, in which they have confronted evil and must incorporate it into their understanding of the world. As a result of this portrayal of the transition from innocence to experience, one of the book's important subthemes involves the threat that hatred, prejudice, and ignorance pose to the innocent: people such as Tom Robinson and Boo Radley are not prepared for the evil that they encounter, and, as a result, they are destroyed. Even Jem is victimized to an extent by his discovery of the evil of racism during and after the trial. Whereas Scout is able to maintain her basic faith in human nature despite Tom's conviction, Jem's faith in justice and in humanity is badly damaged, and he retreats into a state of disillusionment.

The moral voice of *To Kill a Mockingbird* is embodied by Atticus Finch, who is virtually unique in the novel in that he has experienced and understood evil without losing his faith in the human capacity for goodness. Atticus understands that, rather than being simply creatures of good or creatures of evil, most people have both good and bad qualities. The important thing is to appreciate the good qualities and understand the bad qualities by treating others with sympathy and trying to see life from their perspective. He tries to teach this ultimate moral lesson to Jem and Scout to show them that it is possible to live with conscience without losing hope or becoming cynical. In this way, Atticus is able to admire Mrs. Dubose's courage even while deploring her racism. Scout's progress as a character

in the novel is defined by her gradual development toward understanding Atticus's lessons, culminating when, in the final chapters,
Scout at last sees Boo Radley as a human being. Her newfound ability to view the world from his perspective ensures that she will not
become jaded as she loses her innocence.

The Importance of Moral Education

Because exploration of the novel's larger moral questions takes
place within the perspective of children, the education of children is
necessarily involved in the development of all of the novel's themes.
In a sense, the plot of the story charts Scout's moral education, and
the theme of how children are educated—how they are taught to
move from innocence to adulthood—recurs throughout the novel
(at the end of the book, Scout even says that she has learned practi-
cally everything except algebra). This theme is explored most pow-
erfully through the relationship between Atticus and his children, as
he devotes himself to instilling a social conscience in Jem and Scout.
The scenes at school provide a direct counterpoint to Atticus's effective education of his children: Scout is frequently confronted with
teachers who are either frustratingly unsympathetic to children's
needs or morally hypocritical. As is true of *To Kill a Mockingbird*'s
other moral themes, the novel's conclusion about education is that
the most important lessons are those of sympathy and understanding, and that a sympathetic, understanding approach is the best way
to teach these lessons. In this way, Atticus's ability to put himself
in his children's shoes makes him an excellent teacher, while Miss
Caroline's rigid commitment to the educational techniques that she
learned in college makes her ineffective and even dangerous.

The Existence of Social Inequality

Differences in social status are explored largely through the over-
complicated social hierarchy of Maycomb, the ins and outs of
which constantly baffle the children. The relatively well-off Finches
stand near the top of Maycomb's social hierarchy, with most of the
townspeople beneath them. Ignorant country farmers like the Cunninghams lie below the townspeople, and the poor white Ewells rest
below the Cunninghams. But the black community in Maycomb,
despite its abundance of admirable qualities, squats below even the
Ewells, enabling Bob Ewell to make up for his own lack of importance by persecuting Tom Robinson. These rigid social divisions
that make up so much of the adult world are revealed in the book
to be both irrational and destructive. For example, Scout cannot

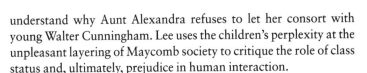

understand why Aunt Alexandra refuses to let her consort with young Walter Cunningham. Lee uses the children's perplexity at the unpleasant layering of Maycomb society to critique the role of class status and, ultimately, prejudice in human interaction.

MOTIFS

Motifs are recurring structures, contrasts, and literary devices that can help to develop and inform the text's major themes.

GOTHIC DETAILS

The forces of good and evil in *To Kill a Mockingbird* seem larger than the small Southern town in which the story takes place. Lee adds drama and atmosphere to her story by including a number of Gothic details in the setting and the plot. In literature, the term Gothic refers to a style of fiction first popularized in eighteenth-century England, featuring supernatural occurrences, gloomy and haunted settings, full moons, and so on. Among the Gothic elements in *To Kill a Mockingbird* are the unnatural snowfall, the fire that destroys Miss Maudie's house, the children's superstitions about Boo Radley, the mad dog that Atticus shoots, and the ominous night of the Halloween party on which Bob Ewell attacks the children. These elements, out of place in the normally quiet, predictable Maycomb, create tension in the novel and serve to foreshadow the troublesome events of the trial and its aftermath.

SMALL-TOWN LIFE

Counterbalancing the Gothic motif of the story is the motif of old-fashioned, small-town values, which manifest themselves throughout the novel. As if to contrast with all of the suspense and moral grandeur of the book, Lee emphasizes the slow-paced, good-natured feel of life in Maycomb. She often deliberately juxtaposes small-town values and Gothic images in order to examine more closely the forces of good and evil. The horror of the fire, for instance, is mitigated by the comforting scene of the people of Maycomb banding together to save Miss Maudie's possessions. In contrast, Bob Ewell's cowardly attack on the defenseless Scout, who is dressed like a giant ham for the school pageant, shows him to be unredeemably evil.

SYMBOLS

Symbols are objects, characters, figures, and colors used to represent abstract ideas or concepts.

MOCKINGBIRDS

The title of *To Kill a Mockingbird* has very little literal connection to the plot, but it carries a great deal of symbolic weight in the book. In this story of innocents destroyed by evil, the "mockingbird" comes to represent the idea of innocence. Thus, to kill a mockingbird is to destroy innocence. Throughout the book, a number of characters (Jem, Tom Robinson, Dill, Boo Radley, Mr. Raymond) can be identified as mockingbirds—innocents who have been injured or destroyed through contact with evil. This connection between the novel's title and its main theme is made explicit several times in the novel: after Tom Robinson is shot, Mr. Underwood compares his death to "the senseless slaughter of songbirds," and at the end of the book Scout thinks that hurting Boo Radley would be like "shootin' a mockingbird." Most important, Miss Maudie explains to Scout: "Mockingbirds don't do one thing but . . . sing their hearts out for us. That's why it's a sin to kill a mockingbird." That Jem and Scout's last name is Finch (another type of small bird) indicates that they are particularly vulnerable in the racist world of Maycomb, which often treats the fragile innocence of childhood harshly.

BOO RADLEY

As the novel progresses, the children's changing attitude toward Boo Radley is an important measurement of their development from innocence toward a grown-up moral perspective. At the beginning of the book, Boo is merely a source of childhood superstition. As he leaves Jem and Scout presents and mends Jem's pants, he gradually becomes increasingly and intriguingly real to them. At the end of the novel, he becomes fully human to Scout, illustrating that she has developed into a sympathetic and understanding individual. Boo, an intelligent child ruined by a cruel father, is one of the book's most important mockingbirds; he is also an important symbol of the good that exists within people. Despite the pain that Boo has suffered, the purity of his heart rules his interaction with the children. In saving Jem and Scout from Bob Ewell, Boo proves the ultimate symbol of good.

SUMMARY & ANALYSIS

PART ONE, CHAPTER 1

SUMMARY

The story is narrated by a young girl named Jean Louise Finch, who is almost always called by her nickname, Scout. Scout starts to explain the circumstances that led to the broken arm that her older brother, Jem, sustained many years earlier; she begins by recounting her family history. The first of her ancestors to come to America was a fur-trader and apothecary named Simon Finch, who fled England to escape religious persecution and established a successful farm on the banks of the Alabama River. The farm, called Finch's Landing, supported the family for many years. The first Finches to make a living away from the farm were Scout's father, Atticus Finch, who became a lawyer in the nearby town of Maycomb, and his brother, Jack Finch, who went to medical school in Boston. Their sister, Alexandra Finch, stayed to run the Landing.

A successful lawyer, Atticus makes a solid living in Maycomb, a tired, poor, old town in the grips of the Great Depression. He lives with Jem and Scout on Maycomb's main residential street. Their cook, an old black woman named Calpurnia, helps to raise the children and keep the house. Atticus's wife died when Scout was two, so she does not remember her mother well. But Jem, four years older than Scout, has memories of their mother that sometimes make him unhappy.

In the summer of 1933, when Jem is nearly ten and Scout almost six, a peculiar boy named Charles Baker Harris moves in next door. The boy, who calls himself Dill, stays for the summer with his aunt, Miss Rachel Haverford, who owns the house next to the Finches'. Dill doesn't like to discuss his father's absence from his life, but he is otherwise a talkative and extremely intelligent boy who quickly becomes the Finch children's chief playmate. All summer, the three act out various stories that they have read. When they grow bored of this activity, Dill suggests that they attempt to lure Boo Radley, a mysterious neighbor, out of his house.

Arthur "Boo" Radley lives in the run-down Radley Place, and no one has seen him outside it in years. Scout recounts how, as a boy,

Boo got in trouble with the law and his father imprisoned him in the house as punishment. He was not heard from until fifteen years later, when he stabbed his father with a pair of scissors. Although people suggested that Boo was crazy, old Mr. Radley refused to have his son committed to an asylum. When the old man died, Boo's brother, Nathan, came to live in the house with Boo. Nevertheless, Boo continued to stay inside.

Dill is fascinated by Boo and tries to convince the Finch children to help him lure this phantom of Maycomb outside. Eventually, he dares Jem to run over and touch the house. Jem does so, sprinting back hastily; there is no sign of movement at the Radley Place, although Scout thinks that she sees a shutter move slightly, as if someone were peeking out.

ANALYSIS

> There was no hurry, for there was nowhere to go, nothing to buy and no money to buy it with, nothing to see outside the boundaries of Maycomb County. But it was a time of vague optimism for some of the people: Maycomb County had recently been told that it had nothing to fear but fear itself.
>
> (See QUOTATIONS, p. 55)

The story that constitutes almost the entirety of *To Kill a Mockingbird* is set in the time between Scout Finch's fifth and ninth birthdays, but Scout presumably commences the first-person narrative that opens the novel much later in her life. As a result, the narrative voice fluctuates between the child's point of view, chronicling the events as they happen, and the adult voice, looking back on her childhood many years later. The child's naïve voice dominates the central plot, allowing the reader to make connections and understand events in a way that the young Scout does not. At the same time, the narrative often digresses into anecdotes or descriptions presented retrospectively, like Scout's depiction of Maycomb in the first chapter: "Maycomb was an old town, but it was a tired old town when I first knew it. . . . Somehow, it was hotter then . . . [p]eople moved slowly then." Here, Lee's language indicates an adult's recollection rather than a girl's experience.

Structurally, *To Kill a Mockingbird* is circular: the story begins where it ends. The first line of the novel introduces Jem's broken arm, and the novel then flashes back to cover the events leading up to his accident. The narrator uses this device to provide background for the Finch family, introducing the legendary Simon Finch and his three descendants. But at this stage of the novel, the family history is treated as background information, of secondary importance to the private world of the young Finch children. In this way, the first chapter provides only a brief sketch of Atticus, whose importance increases as the novel progresses. Jem and Scout are the center of the story, filling it with their world of imagination and superstition, centered on town myths such as the curious history of Boo Radley and imaginative diversions such as acting out stories from books.

Dill dominates this early part of the novel: he is only a summer visitor, with no connection to Maycomb's adult world. As this adult world asserts itself later in the novel, Dill fades from the story. For now, however, the novel appropriates Dill's childhood perspective and only hints at the darker, more adult problems that will intrude on Jem and Scout. One of the central themes of *To Kill a Mockingbird* is the process of growing up and developing a more mature perspective on life. Correspondingly, the narrative gradually comes to mirror a loss of innocence, as the carefree childhood of this first chapter is slowly replaced by a darker, more dangerous, and more cynical adult story in which the children are only minor participants.

Boo Radley becomes the focus of the children's curiosity in Chapter 1. As befits the perspective of childhood innocence, the recluse is given no identity apart from the youthful superstitions that surround him: Scout describes him as a "malevolent phantom" over six feet tall who eats squirrels and cats. Of course, the reader realizes that there must be more to Boo's story than these superstitions imply. Eventually, Boo will be transformed from a nightmare villain into a human being, and the children's understanding of him will reflect their own journey toward adulthood.

CHAPTERS 2–3

SUMMARY: CHAPTER 2

September arrives, and Dill leaves Maycomb to return to the town of Meridian. Scout, meanwhile, prepares to go to school for the first time, an event that she has been eagerly anticipating. Once she is finally at school, however, she finds that her teacher, Miss Caroline Fisher, deals poorly with children. When Miss Caroline concludes that Atticus must have taught Scout to read, she becomes very displeased and makes Scout feel guilty for being educated. At recess, Scout complains to Jem, but Jem says that Miss Caroline is just trying out a new method of teaching.

Miss Caroline and Scout get along badly in the afternoon as well. Walter Cunningham, a boy in Scout's class, has not brought a lunch. Miss Caroline offers him a quarter to buy lunch, telling him that he can pay her back tomorrow. Walter's family is large and poor—so poor that they pay Atticus with hickory nuts, turnip greens, or other goods when they need legal help—and Walter will never be able to pay the teacher back or bring a lunch to school. When Scout attempts to explain these circumstances, however, Miss Caroline fails to understand and grows so frustrated that she slaps Scout's hand with a ruler.

SUMMARY: CHAPTER 3

At lunch, Scout rubs Walter's nose in the dirt for getting her in trouble, but Jem intervenes and invites Walter to lunch (in the novel, as in certain regions of the country, the midday meal is called "dinner"). At the Finch house, Walter and Atticus discuss farm conditions "like two men," and Walter puts molasses all over his meat and vegetables, to Scout's horror. When she criticizes Walter, however, Calpurnia calls her into the kitchen to scold her and slaps her as she returns to the dining room, telling her to be a better hostess. Back at school, Miss Caroline becomes terrified when a tiny bug, or "cootie," crawls out of a boy's hair. The boy is Burris Ewell, a member of the Ewell clan, which is even poorer and less respectable than the Cunningham clan. In fact, Burris only comes to school the first day of every school year, making a token appearance to avoid trouble with the law. He leaves the classroom, making enough vicious remarks to cause the teacher to cry.

At home, Atticus follows Scout outside to ask her if something is wrong, to which she responds that she is not feeling well. She tells him that she does not think she will go to school anymore and suggests that he could teach her himself. Atticus replies that the law demands that she go to school, but he promises to keep reading to her, as long as she does not tell her teacher about it.

You never really understand a person until you . . .
climb into his skin and walk around in it.

(See QUOTATIONS, *p. 56*)

ANALYSIS: CHAPTERS 2–3

Scout's unpleasant first day of school has a threefold purpose: it locates the reader's sympathies firmly with the narrator; it offers a further introduction to Maycomb's tortured social ladder; and it provides sharp social commentary on the theme of children and education, one of the book's most important themes. In her interactions with Miss Caroline, Scout is victimized by her teacher's inexperience; Scout means well but receives only punishment in return. The rigid, impersonal protocols demanded by the law and by Miss Caroline's method of teaching are shown to be insufficient and irrational—Burris Ewell can keep the law happy by coming to school only one day a year, while Scout incurs her teacher's wrath simply by learning to read at an early age. This topsy-turvy educational outlook fails catastrophically to meet the needs of either student. Scout, who is commonsensical enough to perceive this failure immediately, is frustrated by her inability to understand why her teacher acts as she does, and why she, Scout, continually incurs disfavor for well-intentioned actions.

Throughout these chapters, Scout's well-meaning missteps (telling the teacher about Walter's poverty, criticizing Walter for putting molasses on his meat and vegetables) earn harsh rebukes from the adult world, emphasizing the contrast between the comfortable, imaginative childhood world that Scout occupies in Chapter 1 and the more grown-up world she is now expected to occupy. This interaction sets a pattern for the book and for the basic development of Scout as a character: whether dealing with adults or with other children, Scout always means well, and her nature is essentially good. Her mistakes are honest mistakes, and while there is evil all around her in the novel, it does not infect her, nor does injustice disillusion her, as it does Jem. At the end of Chapter 2, Scout, acting on her best intentions (as always), tries to explain the Cunninghams to Miss Caroline.

Young Walter Cunningham is the first glimpse we get of the Cunningham clan, part of the large population of poor farmers in the land around Maycomb. Walter's poverty introduces the very adult theme of social class into the novel. Scout notes in Chapter 1 that

Maycomb was a run-down town caught up in the Great Depression, but so far, we have seen only the upper-class side of town, represented by relatively successful and comfortable characters such as Atticus. Now, however, we begin to see the rest of Maycomb, represented by the struggling Cunninghams and the dirt-poor Ewells. Jem later divides Maycomb into four social classes, placing the Cunninghams a level beneath the other families in the town (Walter's fondness for molasses on all of his food illustrates the difference in status between his family and the Finches).

A correlation between social status and moral goodness becomes evident as the novel progresses. At the top of this pyramid rests Atticus, a comparatively wealthy man whose moral standing is beyond reproach. Beneath him are the poor farmers such as the Cunninghams. The Ewells are below even the Cunninghams on the social ladder, and their unapologetic, squalid ignorance and ill tempers quickly make them the villains of the story. We do not encounter them again until Part Two, but Burris's vicious cruelty in this section foreshadows the later behavior of his father, Bob Ewell.

Miss Caroline's teaching methods, meanwhile, facilitate Lee's subtle critique of educational orthodoxy. Miss Caroline cannot accept that Scout already knows how to read and write, because it confounds the teaching formula that she has been taught to implement. She adheres strictly to a "method" that she learned from adults, instead of learning from her experiences in the classroom and adapting her teaching accordingly. To Scout, this method is dull; to the reader, it exemplifies how well-meaning but rigid thinking can fail. Just as Atticus encourages Scout to place herself in another person's position before she judges that person, Miss Caroline would do better to try to think like her students and respond to their needs rather than simply trying to impose an external system on their education. Throughout the novel, Atticus's moral position of sympathy and understanding is contrasted with rigid, impersonal systems such as Miss Caroline's that fail to account for individual necessities. In this sense, Miss Caroline's behavior in the schoolhouse foreshadows the courtroom scenes later in the novel, when the system that fails is not an educational technique but the law.

Chapters 4–6

Summary: Chapter 4

The rest of the school year passes grimly for Scout, who endures a curriculum that moves too slowly and leaves her constantly frustrated in class. After school one day, she passes the Radley Place and sees some tinfoil sticking out of a knothole in one of the Radleys' oak trees. Scout reaches into the knothole and discovers two pieces of chewing gum. She chews both pieces and tells Jem about it. He panics and makes her spit it out. On the last day of school, however, they find two old "Indian-head" pennies hidden in the same knothole where Scout found the gum and decide to keep them.

Summer comes at last, school ends, and Dill returns to Maycomb. He, Scout, and Jem begin their games again. One of the first things they do is roll one another inside an old tire. On Scout's turn, she rolls in front of the Radley steps, and Jem and Scout panic. However, this incident gives Jem the idea for their next game: they will play "Boo Radley." As the summer passes, their game becomes more complicated, until they are acting out an entire Radley family melodrama. Eventually, however, Atticus catches them and asks if their game has anything to do with the Radleys. Jem lies, and Atticus goes back into the house. The kids wonder if it's safe to play their game anymore.

Summary: Chapter 5

Jem and Dill grow closer, and Scout begins to feel left out of their friendship. As a result, she starts spending much of her time with one of their neighbors: Miss Maudie Atkinson, a widow with a talent for gardening and cake baking who was a childhood friend of Atticus's brother, Jack. She tells Scout that Boo Radley is still alive and it is her theory Boo is the victim of a harsh father (now deceased), a "foot-washing" Baptist who believed that most people are going to hell. Miss Maudie adds that Boo was always polite and friendly as a child. She says that most of the rumors about him are false, but that if he wasn't crazy as a boy, he probably is by now.

Meanwhile, Jem and Dill plan to give a note to Boo inviting him out to get ice cream with them. They try to stick the note in a window of the Radley Place with a fishing pole, but Atticus catches them and orders them to "stop tormenting that man" with either notes or the "Boo Radley" game.

SUMMARY: CHAPTER 6

Jem and Dill obey Atticus until Dill's last day in Maycomb, when he and Jem plan to sneak over to the Radley Place and peek in through a loose shutter. Scout accompanies them, and they creep around the house, peering in through various windows. Suddenly, they see the shadow of a man with a hat on and flee, hearing a shotgun go off behind them. They escape under the fence by the schoolyard, but Jem's pants get caught on the fence, and he has to kick them off in order to free himself.

The children return home, where they encounter a collection of neighborhood adults, including Atticus, Miss Maudie, and Miss Stephanie Crawford, the neighborhood gossip. Miss Maudie informs them that Mr. Nathan Radley shot at "a Negro" in his yard. Miss Stephanie adds that Mr. Radley is waiting outside with his gun so he can shoot at the next sound he hears. When Atticus asks Jem where his pants are, Dill interjects that he won Jem's pants in a game of strip poker. Alarmed, Atticus asks them if they were playing cards. Jem responds that they were just playing with matches. Late that night, Jem sneaks out to the Radley Place, and retrieves his pants.

ANALYSIS: CHAPTERS 4–6

These chapters serve primarily as a record of Jem and Scout's childhood adventures with Dill and the specter of Boo Radley. Even as the children play the "Boo Radley game," make their attempts to give a message to Boo, and peek through his shutters, Boo's character is transformed from a monster into a human being. Although Boo's relevance to the main plot of the novel is still unknown, the compelling human story that these chapters weave around Boo keeps the reader interested in him, even if he serves only as a diversion to the young Finch children at this point.

Boo makes his presence felt in these chapters in a number of ways. First, the presents begin to appear in the Radley tree, and, though Scout does not realize who has been putting them there, the reader can easily guess that it is Boo. Second, Miss Maudie offers insight into the origins of Boo's reclusiveness and a sympathetic perspective on his story. Miss Maudie has only contempt for the superstitious view of Boo: he is no demon, and she knows that he is alive, because she hasn't seen him "carried out yet." From her point of view, Boo was a nice boy who suffered at the hands of a tyrannically religious family. He is one of many victims populating a book whose title, *To Kill a Mockingbird*, suggests the destruction of an innocent being. In fact, as a sweet, young child apparently driven mad by an overbearing father obsessed with sin and retribution, Boo epitomizes the loss of innocence that the book, as a whole, dramatizes. For the children, who first treat him as a superstition and an object of ridicule but later come to view him as a human being, Boo becomes an important benchmark in their gradual development of a more sympathetic, mature perspective.

In these chapters, the first person other than Atticus to display a sympathetic attitude toward Boo is Miss Maudie, who, like Boo, emerges as an important character in this section. Miss Maudie is one of the book's strongest, most resilient female characters. One of the few people in the town who share Atticus's sense of justice, she is also Scout's closest friend and confidante among the local women. Atticus's wife is dead, leaving Scout with Miss Maudie and Aunt Alexandra as her principal maternal figures. Whereas the latter provides a vision of proper womanhood and family pride, the former offers Scout understanding instead of criticizing her for wearing pants and not being ladylike. Miss Maudie is a stronger role model for Scout: she serves as a conscience for the town's women, just as Atticus does for the men, and her sharp tongue and honesty make her the opposite of vapid gossips like Stephanie Crawford.

CHAPTERS 7–8

SUMMARY: CHAPTER 7

A few days later, after school has begun for the year, Jem tells Scout that he found the pants mysteriously mended and hung neatly over the fence. When they come home from school that day, they find another present hidden in the knothole: a ball of gray twine. They leave it there for a few days, but no one takes it, so they claim it for their own.

Unsurprisingly, Scout is as unhappy in second grade as she was in first, but Jem promises her that school gets better the farther along one goes. Late that fall, another present appears in the knothole— two figures carved in soap to resemble Scout and Jem. The figures are followed in turn by chewing gum, a spelling bee medal, and an old pocket watch. The next day, Jem and Scout find that the knothole has been filled with cement. When Jem asks Mr. Radley (Nathan Radley, Boo's brother) about the knothole the following day, Mr. Radley replies that he plugged the knothole because the tree is dying.

SUMMARY: CHAPTER 8

For the first time in years, Maycomb endures a real winter. There is even light snowfall, an event rare enough for school to be closed. Jem and Scout haul as much snow as they could from Miss Maudie's yard to their own. Since there is not enough snow to make a real snowman, they build a small figure out of dirt and cover it with snow. They make it look like Mr. Avery, an unpleasant man who lives down the street. The figure's likeness to Mr. Avery is so strong that Atticus demands that they disguise it. Jem places Miss Maudie's sunhat on its head and sticks her hedge clippers in its hands, much to her chagrin.

That night, Atticus wakes Scout and helps her put on her bathrobe and coat and goes outside with her and Jem. Miss Maudie's house is on fire. The neighbors help her save her furniture, and the fire truck arrives in time to stop the fire from spreading to other houses, but Miss Maudie's house burns to the ground. In the confusion, someone drapes a blanket over Scout. When Atticus later asks her about it, she has no idea who put it over her. Jem realizes that Boo Radley put it on her, and he reveals the whole story of the knothole, the presents, and the mended pants to Atticus. Atticus tells them to keep it to themselves, and Scout, realizing that Boo was just behind her, nearly throws up.

Despite having lost her house, Miss Maudie is cheerful the next day. She tells the children how much she hated her old home and that she is already planning to build a smaller house and plant a larger garden. She says that she wishes she had been there when Boo put the blanket on Scout to catch him in the act.

ANALYSIS: CHAPTERS 7–8

Originally portrayed as a freak and a lunatic, Boo Radley continues to gain the sympathy of the children in these chapters. Lee uses an elliptical technique in telling Boo's story—she hints and implies at what is happening without ever showing the reader directly. The reader must read between the lines—inferring, for instance, that it was Boo Radley who mended Jem's pants and placed the presents in the tree, since Scout does not realize that Boo's hand is at work until Jem explains things to Atticus after the fire.

In comparison to Scout's still very childish perspective, Jem's more mature understanding of the world is evident here, along with his strong sense of justice. When Nathan Radley plugs up the hole in the tree, Scout is disappointed but hardly heartbroken, seeing it as merely the end of their presents. Jem, on the other hand, is brought to tears, because he grasps that Boo's brother has done something cruel: he has deprived Boo of his connection to the wider world and has broken up his brother's attempt at friendship. This incident, which the reader must detect behind the scenes of Scout's narrative, plays into the novel's broad theme of suffering innocence, and Jem's anger at this injustice foreshadows his later fury concerning Tom Robinson's trial. While Scout retains her innocence and optimism throughout the book, Jem undergoes severe disillusionment as part of his "growing up," and the Boo Radley incident in this chapter is an important early step toward that disillusionment.

The implicit comparison between Boo's soap figures and Jem and Scout's snowman reveals the difference in how each party interacts with others. Whereas Boo carves his figures out of a desire to connect with the two kids, Jem and Scout craft their snowman out of a dislike for Mr. Avery. Further, Boo doesn't make his carvings for himself; rather, he offers them as presents. Jem and Scout, on the other hand, make the snowman purely for their own enjoyment. Boo interacts with others on their terms, while the children, not yet mature, interact with others on their own terms.

Critic Claudia Durst Johnson has argued that *To Kill a Mockingbird* contains many Gothic elements, from the legends and secrets surrounding Boo Radley to Dill's imaginative stories and the children's superstitions. The unseasonable snow and the fire at Miss Maudie's, as well as the later appearance of a mad dog, can be seen as contributing to a sense of supernatural foreboding leading up to the injustice that pervades Tom Robinson's trial. This interpretation, however, is balanced by the fact that both the snow and the fire bring out the best in people—school is canceled, Scout and Jem build a fine snowman, the neighbors help save Miss Maudie's belongings, and Miss Maudie perseveres after her house is destroyed. Even when she sees her prize flowers ruined, the brave old woman does not despair; instead, she offers a cheerful comment about wanting a smaller house and a larger garden. This interweaving of dramatic, Gothic atmospherics and good-hearted small-town values epitomizes *To Kill a Mockingbird* and mirrors the novel's main theme. In a world in which innocence is threatened by injustice, cruelty, prejudice, and hatred, goodness can prevail in the form of sympathy, understanding, and common sense, as evidenced by how the townspeople's affectionate willingness to help one another enables them to overcome the intrusion of these Gothic elements into their simple small-town lives.

Chapters 9–11

Summary: Chapter 9

At school, Scout nearly starts a fight with a classmate named Cecil Jacobs after Cecil declares that "Scout Finch's daddy defends niggers." Atticus has been asked to defend Tom Robinson, a black man accused of raping a white woman. It is a case he cannot hope to win, but he tells Scout that he must argue it to uphold his sense of justice and self-respect.

At Christmastime, Atticus's brother, Jack, comes to stay with Atticus for a week during the holidays. Scout generally gets along well with Uncle Jack, but when he arrives in Maycomb, she begins cursing in front of him (a habit that she has recently picked up). After supper, Jack has Scout sit on his lap and he warns her not to curse in his presence. On Christmas Day, Atticus takes his children and Jack to Finch's Landing, a rambling old house in the country where Atticus's sister, Alexandra, and her husband live. There, Scout endures Francis, Alexandra's grandson, who had been dropped off at Finch's Landing for the holiday. Scout thinks Francis is the most "boring" child she has ever met. She also has to put up with the prim and proper Alexandra, who insists that Scout dress like a lady instead of wearing pants.

One night, Francis tells Scout that Dill is a runt and then calls Atticus a "nigger-lover." Scout curses him and beats him up. Francis tells Alexandra and Uncle Jack that Scout hit him, and Uncle Jack spanks her without hearing her side of the story. After they return to Maycomb, Scout tells Jack what Francis said and Jack becomes furious. Scout makes him promise not to tell Atticus, however, because Atticus had asked her not to fight anyone over what is said about him. Jack promises and keeps his word. Later, Scout overhears Atticus telling Jack that Tom Robinson is innocent but doomed, since it's inconceivable that an all-white jury would ever acquit him.

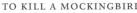

SUMMARY: CHAPTER 10

> *"Mockingbirds don't do one thing but make music for*
> *us to enjoy ... but sing their hearts out for us. That's*
> *why it's a sin to kill a mockingbird."*
>
> *(See* QUOTATIONS, *p. 57)*

Atticus, Scout says, is somewhat older than most of the other fathers in Maycomb. His relatively advanced age often embarrasses his children—he wears glasses and reads, for instance, instead of hunting and fishing like the other men in town. One day, however, a mad dog appears, wandering down the main street toward the Finches' house. Calpurnia calls Atticus, who returns home with Heck Tate, the sheriff of Maycomb. Heck brings a rifle and asks Atticus to shoot the animal. To Jem and Scout's amazement, Atticus does so, hitting the dog with his first shot despite his considerable distance from the dog. Later, Miss Maudie tells Jem and Scout that, as a young man, Atticus was the best shot in the county—"One-shot Finch." Scout is eager to brag about this, but Jem tells her to keep it a secret, because if Atticus wanted them to know, he would have told them.

SUMMARY: CHAPTER 11

On the way to the business district in Maycomb is the house of Mrs. Dubose, a cantankerous old lady who always shouts at Jem and Scout as they pass by. Atticus warns Jem to be a gentleman to her, because she is old and sick, but one day she tells the children that Atticus is not any better than the "niggers and trash he works for," and Jem loses his temper. Jem takes a baton from Scout and destroys all of Mrs. Dubose's camellia bushes. As punishment, Jem must go to her house every day for a month and read to her. Scout accompanies him and they endure Mrs. Dubose's abuse and peculiar fits, which occur at the end of every reading session. Each session is longer than the one before. Mrs. Dubose dies a little more than a month after Jem's punishment ends. Atticus reveals to Jem that she was addicted to morphine and that the reading was part of her successful effort to combat this addiction. Atticus gives Jem a box that Mrs. Dubose had given her maid for Jem; in it lies a single white camellia.

ANALYSIS: CHAPTERS 9–11

The fire in which the previous section culminated represents an important turning point in the narrative structure of *To Kill a*

Mockingbird. Before the fire, the novel centers on Scout's childhood world, the games that she plays with Jem and Dill, and their childhood superstitions about Boo Radley. After the fire, Boo Radley and childhood pursuits begin to retreat from the story, and the drama of the trial takes over. This shift begins the novel's gradual dramatization of the loss-of-innocence theme, as adult problems and concerns begin disrupting the happy world of the Finch children.

The occasion for the adult world to intrude on Scout's life is the trial of Tom Robinson. Because Robinson is a black man accused of raping a white woman, the white residents of Maycomb are furious that Atticus, the town's best lawyer, would choose to help his cause. The townspeople are unwilling to limit their displays of anger to Atticus himself; Scout and Jem become targets as well. The town of Maycomb, whose inhabitants have been presented thus far in a largely positive light, suddenly turns against the Finches, as the ugly, racist underbelly of Southern life exposes itself. Even members of Atticus's own family—Alexandra and her obnoxious grandson—condemn his decision to defend Tom Robinson. Chapter 9 marks Alexandra's first appearance in the story, and her portrayal is mostly negative; only later will she develop into a sympathetic character.

The adversity faced by the family reveals Atticus's parenting style, his focus on instilling moral values in Jem and Scout. Particularly important to Atticus are justice, restraint, and honesty. He tells his children to avoid getting in fights, even if they are verbally abused, and to practice quiet courage instead. When he gives Jem and Scout air rifles as presents, he advises them that it is a sin to kill a mockingbird. This idea is, of course, the source of the novel's title, and it reflects the book's preoccupation with injustices inflicted upon innocents. In different ways, Jem and Scout, Boo Radley, and Tom Robinson are all "mockingbirds."

The incident with the mad dog demonstrates Atticus's courage and symbolizes the town's dependence upon his protection from both the rabid animal and the worst evil within themselves. That Scout, in particular, is so impressed with the masculine prowess with which she associates his marksmanship symbolizes how much she has to learn about courage. For, in Atticus's mind, true bravery has nothing to do with weapons. The subsequent events surrounding Mrs. Dubose give him an opportunity to show Jem what he considers real courage. Mrs. Dubose, in many ways, represents everything wrong with Maycomb: she is unforgivably racist, raining curses on the children and denigrating Atticus for representing a black man. Yet the darkness in her is balanced by her bravery and determination, and just as Atticus loves Maycomb despite its flaws, he respects Mrs. Dubose for possessing "real courage," which he explains as "when you know you're licked before you begin but you begin anyway and you see it through no matter what." This attitude, of course, fittingly describes Atticus's approach to the Tom Robinson case. Atticus puts into practice every moral idea that he espouses, which is the key to his importance in Maycomb and his heroism in the novel.

The camellia that Mrs. Dubose leaves Jem constitutes a distillation of what Atticus considers her essential goodness. She has sloughed off her mortal persona, one that is racist and irritable, and the whiteness of the flower symbolizes the purity of soul that Atticus attributes to everyone. Jem's initial rejection of the gift symbolizes his inability to see this goodness. Although Mrs. Dubose's gesture seems to imply an appreciation of Jem, Jem has not yet matured enough to realize that good and evil can coexist within the same person; he thus remains unwilling to accept that Mrs. Dubose could represent anything good.

PART TWO, CHAPTERS 12–13

SUMMARY: CHAPTER 12

By this time, Jem has reached the age of twelve, and he begins to demand that Scout "stop pestering him" and act more like a girl. Scout becomes upset and looks forward desperately to Dill's arrival in the summer. To Scout's disappointment, however, Dill does not come to Maycomb this year. He sends a letter saying that he has a new father (presumably, his mother has remarried) and will stay with his family in Meridian. To make matters worse, the state legislature, of which Atticus is a member, is called into session, forcing Atticus to travel to the state capital every day for two weeks.

Calpurnia decides to take the children to her church, a "colored" church, that Sunday. Maycomb's black church is an old building, called First Purchase because it was bought with the first earnings of freed slaves. One woman, Lula, criticizes Calpurnia for bringing white children to church, but the congregation is generally friendly, and Reverend Sykes welcomes them, saying that everyone knows their father. The church has no money for hymnals, and few of the parishioners can read, so they sing by echoing the words that Zeebo, Calpurnia's eldest son and the town garbage collector, reads from their only hymnal. During the service, Reverend Sykes takes up a collection for Tom Robinson's wife, Helen, who cannot find work now that her husband has been accused of rape. After the service, Scout learns that Tom Robinson has been accused by Bob Ewell and cannot understand why anyone would believe the Ewells' word. When the children return home, they find Aunt Alexandra waiting for them.

SUMMARY: CHAPTER 13

Aunt Alexandra explains that she should stay with the children for a while, to give them a "feminine influence." Maycomb gives her a fine welcome: various ladies in the town bake her cakes and have her over for coffee, and she soon becomes an integral part of the town's social life. Alexandra is extremely proud of the Finches and spends much of her time discussing the characteristics of the various families in Maycomb. This "family consciousness" is an integral part of life in Maycomb, an old town where the same families have lived for generations, where every family has its quirks and eccentricities. However, Jem and Scout lack the pride that Aunt Alexandra considers commensurate with being a Finch. She orders Atticus to lecture them on the subject of their ancestry. He makes a valiant attempt but succeeds only in making Scout cry.

ANALYSIS: CHAPTERS 12–13

Dill's absence from Maycomb coincides appropriately with the continued encroachment of the adult world upon Scout's childhood, as Dill has represented the perspective of childhood throughout the novel. Scout's journey to Calpurnia's church is the reader's first glimpse of the black community in Maycomb, which is portrayed in an overwhelmingly positive light. An air of desperate poverty hangs over the church—the building is unpainted, they cannot afford hymnals, and the congregation is illiterate—yet the adversity seems to bring the people closer together and creates a stronger sense of community than is found in Scout's own church. The devotion of the black church contrasts starkly with the hypocrisy of the white ladies' missionary circle that Scout attends in Chapter 24. There, one of the missionary ladies, Mrs. Merriweather, bemoans the plight of the oppressed indigenous people of Africa at the same time that she complains about how moody Maycomb's blacks are.

In addition, Lee introduces the black community at a crucial moment in the narrative—just as race relations in Maycomb are thrown into crisis by the trial of Tom Robinson. By emphasizing the goodness and solidarity of the black community, Lee casts the racism rampant among Maycomb's whites in an extremely harsh and ugly light. One of the main moral themes of the novel is that of sympathy and understanding, Atticus's tenet that Scout should always try to put herself in someone else's shoes before she judges them. Lee enables us to identify with the black community in a way that makes the townspeople's unwillingness to do so seem mean-spirited and stubborn. Simply because of their racial prejudice, the townspeople are prepared to accept the word of the cruel, ignorant Bob Ewell over that of a decent black man. If the novel's main theme involves the threat that evil and hatred pose to innocence and goodness, it becomes clear that ignorant, unsympathetic racial prejudice will be the predominant incarnation of evil and hatred, as the childhood innocence of Scout and Jem is thrown into crisis by the circumstances of the trial.

The visit to the church brings Calpurnia to center stage in the novel. Her character serves as the bridge between two worlds, and the reader develops a sense of her double life, which is split between the Finch household and the black community. When she goes to church, her language changes; she speaks in a "colored" dialect rather than the proper, precise language that she uses in Atticus's household. Jem asks her why, and she explains that the churchgoers would think she was "puttin' on airs fit to beat Moses" if she spoke "white" in church. This speech demonstrates the gulf between blacks and whites in Maycomb: not only do class distinctions and bigotry divide the two races, but language does as well.

Aunt Alexandra, meanwhile, takes over the Finch household and imposes her vision of social order. With her rigid notions of class and her habit of declaring what's best for the family, she naturally clashes with Calpurnia, whose presence she deems unnecessary, and Scout, who wants no part of what her aunt represents—namely, respectable Southern womanhood. The reader may side with Scout at this juncture and consider Aunt Alexandra inflexible and narrow-minded, but (like most of the book's characters) she has many redeeming qualities. She may not have her brother's fierce yearning for justice or his parenting abilities, but her eagerness to rear Jem and Scout properly and her pride in the Finch name demonstrate that she cares deeply about her family.

CHAPTERS 14–15

SUMMARY: CHAPTER 14

The impending trial of Tom Robinson and Atticus's role as his defense lawyer make Jem and Scout the objects of whispers and glances whenever they go to town. One day, Scout tries to ask Atticus what "rape" is, and the subject of the children's trip to Calpurnia's church comes up. Aunt Alexandra tells Scout she cannot go back the next Sunday. Later, she tries to convince Atticus to get rid of Calpurnia, saying that they no longer need her. Atticus refuses. That night, Jem tells Scout not to antagonize Alexandra. Scout gets angry at being lectured and attacks Jem. Atticus breaks up the fight and sends them to bed. Scout discovers something under her bed. She calls Jem in and they discover Dill hiding there.

Dill has run away from home because his mother and new father did not pay enough attention to him. He took a train from Meridian to Maycomb Junction, fourteen miles away, and covered the remaining distance on foot and on the back of a cotton wagon. Jem goes down the hall and tells Atticus. Atticus asks Scout to get more food than a pan of cold corn bread for Dill, before going next door to tell Dill's aunt, Miss Rachel, of his whereabouts. Dill eats, then gets into Jem's bed to sleep, but soon climbs over to Scout's bed to talk things over.

SUMMARY: CHAPTER 15

A week after Dill's arrival, a group of men led by the sheriff, Heck Tate, come to Atticus's house in the evening. As his trial is nearing, Tom Robinson is to be moved to the Maycomb jail, and concerns about the possibility of a lynch mob have arisen. Later, Jem tells Scout that Alexandra and Atticus have been arguing about the trial; she nearly accused him of bringing disgrace on the family. The following evening, Atticus takes the car into town. At about ten o'clock, Jem, accompanied by Scout and Dill, sneaks out of the house and follows his father to the town center. From a distance, they see Atticus sitting in front of the Maycomb jail, reading a newspaper. Jem suggests that they not disturb Atticus and return home.

At that moment, four cars drive into Maycomb and park near the jail. A group of men gets out, and one demands that Atticus move away from the jailhouse door. Atticus refuses, and Scout suddenly comes racing out of her hiding place next door, only to realize that this group of men differs from the group that came to their house the previous night. Jem and Dill follow her, and Atticus orders Jem to go home. Jem refuses, and one of the men tells Atticus that he has fifteen seconds to get his children to leave.

Meanwhile, Scout looks around the group and recognizes Mr. Cunningham, the father of her classmate Walter Cunningham. She starts talking to him about his legal entailments and his son, and asks him to tell his son "hey." All of the men stare at her. Mr. Cunningham, suddenly ashamed, squats down and tells Scout that he will tell his son "hey" for her, and then tells his companions to clear out. They depart, and Mr. Underwood, the owner of the newspaper, speaks from a nearby window where he is positioned with a double-barreled shotgun: "Had you covered all the time, Atticus." Atticus and Mr. Underwood talk for a while, and then Atticus takes the children home.

ANALYSIS: CHAPTERS 14–15

If Aunt Alexandra embodies the rules and customs of the adult world, then the reappearance of Dill at this juncture offers Scout an opportunity to flee, at least for a short time, back into the comforts of childhood. However, Dill's return also emphasizes the growing gulf in development between Scout and Jem. In the previous section, we saw the twelve-year-old Jem indignantly urging Scout to act more like a girl, indicating his growing awareness of adult social roles and expectations. Here again, Jem proves clearly too old for the childhood solidarity that Dill's presence recalls. Scout relates that, upon seeing Dill under the bed, Jem "rose and broke the remaining code of our childhood" by telling Atticus. To Scout, this act makes Jem a "traitor," though it is really an act of responsibility that marks Jem's maturation toward adulthood.

Dill's account of his family troubles reminds both Scout and the reader of the Finch household's good fortune. Atticus is a wonderful father, and Aunt Alexandra's faults result from caring too much rather than too little. Dill's parents have treated him with apathy and disregard, perhaps the greatest offense a parent can commit.

As Scout duly notes, the world of childhood fun that Dill represents can no longer stave off the adult reality of hatred and unfairness that Jem finds himself entering. Whereas, two years before, the Finch children's lives were dominated by games and friendship with Dill, their lives now focus on the adult world of Tom Robinson's trial. The now mature Jem leads Scout and Dill into town on the night that Atticus faces the lynch mob. Symbolically, this scene marks Jem's transition from boy to man, as he stands beside Atticus and refuses to "go home," since only a child would do so. Though he disobeys his father, he does so not petulantly but maturely. He understands Atticus's difficult situation with regard to the case and consequently fears for Atticus's safety. Nevertheless, the confrontation is dominated by Scout's innocence, still sufficiently intact that she can chat with Mr. Cunningham about his son despite being surrounded by a hostile lynch mob.

Some critics find Scout's performance and the dispersal of the mob in this scene unconvincing and pat, wondering how Scout can remain so blissfully unaware of what is really going on and how Mr. Cunningham can be persuaded by Scout's Southern courtesy to break up the drunken posse. Within the moral universe of *To Kill a Mockingbird,* the behavior of both characters makes perfect sense. As befits her innocence, Scout remains convinced of other people's essential goodness, a conviction that the novel shares. Rather than marking them as inherently evil, the mob members' racism only shrouds their humanity, their worthiness, and their essential goodness. Scout's attempt at politeness makes Mr. Cunningham realize her essential goodness, and he responds with civility and kindness. As Atticus says later, the events of that night prove that "a gang of wild animals can be stopped, simply because they're still human."

CHAPTERS 16–17

SUMMARY: CHAPTER 16

The trial begins the next day. People from all over the county flood the town. Everyone makes an appearance in the courtroom, from Miss Stephanie Crawford to Mr. Dolphus Raymond, a wealthy eccentric who owns land on a river bank, lives near the county line, is involved with a black woman, and has mulatto children. Only Miss Maudie refuses to go, saying that watching someone on trial for his life is like attending a Roman carnival.

The vast crowd camps in the town square to eat lunch. Afterward, Jem, Scout, and Dill wait for most of the crowd to enter the courthouse so that they can slip in at the back and thus prevent Atticus from noticing them. However, because they wait too long, they succeed in getting seats only when Reverend Sykes lets them sit in the balcony where black people are required to sit in order to watch the trial. From these seats, they can see the whole courtroom.

Judge Taylor, a white-haired old man with a reputation for running his court in an informal fashion, presides over the case.

SUMMARY: CHAPTER 17

The prosecutor, Mr. Gilmer, questions Heck Tate, who recounts how, on the night of November 21, Bob Ewell urged him to go to the Ewell house and told him that his daughter Mayella had been raped. When Tate got there, he found Mayella bruised and beaten, and she told him that Tom Robinson had raped her. Atticus cross-examines the witness, who admits that no doctor was summoned, and tells Atticus that Mayella's bruises were concentrated on the right side of her face. Tate leaves the stand, and Bob Ewell is called.

Bob Ewell and his children live behind the town garbage dump in a tin-roofed cabin with a yard full of trash. No one is sure how many children Ewell has, and the only orderly corner of the yard is planted with well-tended geraniums rumored to belong to Mayella. An extremely rude little man, Ewell testifies that on the evening in question he was coming out of the woods with a load of kindling when he heard his daughter yelling. When he reached the house, he looked in the window and saw Tom Robinson raping her. Robinson fled, and Ewell went into the house, saw that his daughter was all right, and ran for the sheriff. Atticus's cross-examination is brief: he asks Mr. Ewell why no doctor was called (it was too expensive and there was no need), and then has the witness write his name. Bob Ewell, the jury sees, is left-handed—and a left-handed man would be more likely to leave bruises on the right side of a girl's face.

ANALYSIS: CHAPTERS 16–17

The trial is the most gripping, and in some ways the most important, dramatic sequence in *To Kill a Mockingbird*; the testimony and deliberations cover about five chapters with almost no digression. (Additionally, the courtroom scene, with Atticus picking apart the Ewells as the whole town watches, is the most cinematic portion of the narrative, and it is the centerpiece of the 1962 film version of the novel.) Though the trial targets Tom Robinson, in another sense it is Maycomb that is on trial, and while Atticus eventually loses the court case, he successfully reveals the injustice of a stratified society that confines blacks to the "colored balcony" and allows the word of a despicable, ignorant man like Bob Ewell to prevail without question over the word of a man who happens to be black. In the trial conducted in the courtroom, Atticus loses. In the trial conducted in the mind of the reader, it is the white community, wallowing in prejudice and hatred, that loses.

It is fitting that the children end up sitting in the "colored section" of the courthouse, just as it is fitting that Miss Maudie refuses to attend the trial. All three lack the racism that the crowd of white faces in the courtroom propagates. Jem, Scout, and Dill are segregated even from the other children, who have taunted Jem and Scout with cries of "nigger-lover" in the schoolyard.

That the trial scene creates such an atmosphere of suspense is testimony to the author's skill, because there is no real suspense; even Atticus knows that the verdict is a foregone conclusion. No matter what evidence is presented at the trial, the racist jury would never, under any circumstances, acquit a black man accused of raping a white woman. The reader knows that Tom Robinson will be found guilty, so Lee locates the tension and suspense elsewhere—in Atticus's slow but steady dismantling of the prosecution's case. Jem, still clinging to his youthful illusions about life working according to concepts of fairness, doesn't understand that his father's brilliant efforts will be in vain. He believes that the irrefutable implications of the evidence will clinch the case for Atticus. When Jem says, "We've got him," after Bob Ewell is shown to be left-handed, the reader knows better. Atticus, like Mrs. Dubose in her battle with morphine, is "licked" before he begins.

Bob Ewell's real name is Robert E. Lee Ewell, a moniker that links him with the South's past and makes him absurd by comparison with his namesake, General Robert E. Lee, who fought valiantly for the Confederacy in the Civil War despite his opposition to slavery. If Robert E. Lee represents the idealized South, then Bob Ewell epitomizes its darker and less respectable side, dominated by thoughtless prejudice, squalor, and meanness. Atticus's admonition to Scout that she should increase her tolerance by stepping inside other people's shoes does not apply to Bob Ewell. When Atticus tries to do so later, he only underestimates the depth of this little man's wickedness. The irony, of course, is that Bob Ewell is completely unimportant; he is an arrogant, lazy, abusive fool, laughed at by his fellow townsfolk. Yet in the racist world of Maycomb, sadly, even he has the power to destroy an innocent man—perhaps the novel's most tragic example of the threat posed to innocence by evil.

CHAPTERS 18–19

SUMMARY: CHAPTER 18

The trial continues, with the whole town glued to the proceedings. Mayella, who testifies next, is a reasonably clean—by the Ewells' standards—and obviously terrified nineteen-year-old girl. She says that she called Tom Robinson inside the fence that evening and offered him a nickel to break up a dresser for her, and that once he got inside the house he grabbed her and took advantage of her. In Atticus's cross-examination, Mayella reveals that her life consists of seven unhelpful siblings, a drunken father, and no friends.

Atticus then examines her testimony and asks why she didn't put up a better fight, why her screams didn't bring the other children running, and, most important, how Tom Robinson managed the crime: how he bruised the right side of her face with his useless left hand, which was torn apart by a cotton gin when he was a boy. Atticus pleads with Mayella to admit that there was no rape, that her father beat her. She shouts at him and yells that the courtroom would have to be a bunch of cowards not to convict Tom Robinson; she then bursts into tears, refusing to answer any more questions. In the recess that follows, Mr. Underwood notices the children up in the balcony, but Jem tells Scout that the newspaper editor won't tell Atticus about their being there—although he might include it in the social section of the newspaper. The prosecution rests, and Atticus calls only one witness—Tom Robinson.

SUMMARY: CHAPTER 19

Tom testifies that he always passed the Ewell house on the way to work and that Mayella often asked him to do chores for her. On the evening in question, he recounts, she asked him to come inside the house and fix a door. When he got inside, there was nothing wrong with the door, and he noticed that the other children were gone. Mayella told him she had saved her money and sent them all to buy ice cream. Then she asked him to lift a box down from a dresser. When Tom climbed on a chair, she grabbed his legs, scaring him so much that he jumped down. She then hugged him around the waist and asked him to kiss her. As she struggled, her father appeared at the window, calling Mayella a whore and threatening to kill her. Tom fled.

Link Deas, Tom's white employer, stands up and declares that in eight years of work, he has never had any trouble from Tom.

Judge Taylor furiously expels Deas from the courtroom for inter-
rupting. Mr. Gilmer gets up and cross-examines Tom. The prosecutor points out that the defendant was once arrested for disorderly
conduct and gets Tom to admit that he has the strength, even with
one hand, to choke the breath out of a woman and sling her to the
floor. He begins to badger the witness, asking about his motives
for always helping Mayella with her chores, until Tom declares
that he felt sorry for her. This statement puts the courtroom ill at
ease—in Maycomb, black people aren't supposed to feel sorry for
a white person. Mr. Gilmer reviews Mayella's testimony, accusing
Tom of lying about everything. Dill begins to cry, and Scout takes
him out of the courtroom. Outside the courtroom, Dill complains
to Scout about Mr. Gilmer's rude treatment of Tom Robinson during the questioning. As they walk, Scout and Dill encounter Mr.
Dolphus Raymond, the rich white man with the colored mistress
and mulatto children.

ANALYSIS: CHAPTERS 18–19

Mayella Ewell is pitiable, and her miserable existence almost
allows her to join the novel's parade of innocent victims—she, too,
is a kind of mockingbird, injured beyond repair by the forces of
ugliness, poverty, and hatred that surround her. Lee's presentation
of Mayella emphasizes her role as victim—her father beats her
and possibly molests her, while she has to deal with her unhelpful siblings. She has lacked kind treatment in her life to such an
extent that when Atticus calls her Miss Mayella, she accuses him
of making fun of her. She has no friends, and Scout seems justified
in thinking that she "must have been the loneliest person in the
world." On the other hand, though, Scout's picture of Mayella as a
victim is marred by her attempt to become a victimizer, to destroy
Tom Robinson in order to cover her shame. We can have little real
sympathy for Mayella Ewell—whatever her sufferings, she inflicts
worse cruelty on others. Unlike Mr. Cunningham, who, in Chapter
15, is touched enough by Scout's human warmth to disperse the
lynch mob, Mayella responds to Atticus's polite interrogation with
grouchy snarls.

Pity must be reserved for Tom Robinson, whose honesty and
goodness render him supremely moral. Unlike the Ewells, Tom is
hardworking and honest and has enough compassion to make the
fatal mistake of feeling sorry for Mayella Ewell. His story is the
true version of events: because of both Tom's obviously truthful

nature and Atticus's brilliant and morally scathing questioning of the Ewells, the story leaves no room for doubt. A number of critics have objected that the facts of the case are crafted to be—no pun intended—too black and white. But, as Atticus's awareness of his defeat as a foregone conclusion suggests, Lee was not interested in the believability of the trial. The exaggerated demarcation between good and bad renders the trial more important for its symbolic portrayal of the destruction of an innocent by evil. As clear as it is that Tom is innocent, it is equally clear that Tom is doomed to die.

Link Deas represents the diametric opposite of prejudice. The fact that Tom is black doesn't factor into Deas's assessment of him; rather, he is particularly conscientious about scrutinizing Tom only in respect to his individual character. However, just as the court refuses to accept the undeniable implications of the evidence that Atticus presents, so too does it refuse to accept the implications of Deas's validation of Tom's character. The judge expels Deas because his interjection during the proceedings threatens the integrity of the formal manner in which court proceedings are run; the grim irony, of course, is that the blatant prejudice of the trial does so as well, though the judge does nothing to alleviate this prejudice.

The reader is spared much of Mr. Gilmer's harsh cross-examination of Tom when Dill's crying takes Scout out of the courtroom. Dill is still a child, and he responds to wickedness with tears, much as the reader responds to Mr. Gilmer's unabashed prejudice with disgust. The small sample of his cross-examination that Scout and the reader do hear is enough. Calling Tom "boy" and accusing him at every turn, the racist Mr. Gilmer believes that Tom must be lying, must be violent, must lust after white women—simply because he is black.

CHAPTERS 20–22

SUMMARY: CHAPTER 20

Mr. Dolphus Raymond reveals that he is drinking from a paper sack. He commiserates with Dill and offers him a drink in a paper bag. Dill slurps up some of the liquid and Scout warns him not to take much, but Dill reveals to her that the drink isn't alcoholic—it's only Coca-Cola. Mr. Raymond tells the children that he pretends to be a drunk to provide the other white people with an explanation for his lifestyle, when, in fact, he simply prefers black people to whites.

When Dill and Scout return to the courtroom, Atticus is making his closing remarks. He has finished going over the evidence and now makes a personal appeal to the jury. He points out that the prosecution has produced no medical evidence of the crime and has presented only the shaky testimony of two unreliable witnesses; moreover, the physical evidence suggests that Bob Ewell, not Tom Robinson, beat Mayella. He then offers his own version of events, describing how Mayella, lonely and unhappy, committed the unmentionable act of lusting after a black man and then concealed her shame by accusing him of rape after being caught. Atticus begs the jury to avoid the state's assumption that all black people are criminals and to deliver justice by freeing Tom Robinson. As soon as Atticus finishes, Calpurnia comes into the courtroom.

SUMMARY: CHAPTER 21

Calpurnia hands Atticus a note telling him that his children have not been home since noon. Mr. Underwood says that Jem and Scout are in the colored balcony and have been there since just after one in the afternoon. Atticus tells them to go home and have supper. They beg to be allowed to hear the verdict; Atticus says that they can return after supper, though he knows that the jury will likely have returned before then.

Calpurnia marches Jem, Scout, and Dill home. They eat quickly and return to find the jury still out, the courtroom still full. Evening comes, night falls, and the jury continues to deliberate. Jem is confident of victory, while Dill has fallen asleep. Finally, after eleven that night, the jury enters. Scout remembers that a jury never looks at a man it has convicted, and she notices that the twelve men do not look at Tom Robinson as they file in and deliver a guilty verdict. The courtroom begins to empty, and as Atticus goes out, everyone in the colored balcony rises in a gesture of respect.

SUMMARY: CHAPTER 22

That night, Jem cries, railing against the injustice of the verdict. The next day, Maycomb's black population delivers an avalanche of food to the Finch household. Outside, Miss Stephanie Crawford is gossiping with Mr. Avery and Miss Maudie, and she tries to question Jem and Scout about the trial. Miss Maudie rescues the children by inviting them in for some cake. Jem complains that his illusions about Maycomb have been shattered: he thought that these people were the best in the world, but, having seen the trial, he doesn't think so anymore. Miss Maudie points out that there were people who tried to help, like Judge Taylor, who appointed Atticus to the case instead of the regular public defender. She adds that the jury's staying out so long constitutes a sign of progress in race relations. As the children leave Miss Maudie's house, Miss Stephanie runs over to tell them that Bob Ewell accosted their father that morning, spat on him, and swore revenge.

ANALYSIS: CHAPTERS 20–22

It is easy to criticize Mr. Dolphus Raymond as an unreal, saccharinely nonracist character. Indeed, in a temporal and geographical setting in which the white community as a whole has so little sympathy for blacks, Raymond is not only anomalous but also somewhat preposterous—it seems that even the righteous and morally upstanding Atticus might view Raymond as having breached accepted notions of social propriety. The importance of Raymond's character, however, lies in the nature of his preference for blacks. Raymond never explains precisely why he prefers blacks—he just does; similarly, the white community never explains why it hates blacks—it just does. The difference between these two ingrained attitudes, however, is that whereas the white community imposes its preferences unapologetically on the whole of Maycomb, Raymond acts on his preferences solely because he wants to live that way, not because he wants to dictate how others should live.

Mr. Raymond's presence outside the courtroom is fitting: like Miss Maudie, he does not belong inside with the rest of the white people, because he does not share their guilt. Mr. Raymond is a harsh realist, and while he shares Jem's outrage, he is too old to cry. In a way, Mr. Raymond is another illustration of an innocent destroyed by hatred and prejudice: a moral and conscientious man, he is also an unhappy figure, a good man who has turned cynical and lost hope after witnessing too much evil in the world. "You haven't seen enough of the world yet," he tells Scout, commenting on how special and good her father is, and her innocent belief in human goodness. "You haven't even seen this town, but all you gotta do is step back inside the courthouse."

Whereas Mr. Raymond believes that Maycomb's racist side is the real Maycomb, Atticus, less embittered, seems to hold out hope for the town—significantly, his eloquent closing argument is devoid of despair. Rather, he speaks to the jury with confidence and dignity, urging them to find confidence and dignity within themselves. Though *To Kill a Mockingbird* dramatizes the threat posed to goodness by evil, and though it frequently treats this theme by exploring the destruction of innocence, the novel's ultimate moral outlook is not bleak; rather, it is characterized by Atticus's wise understanding of both the goodness and the badness within people. Moral issues within the novel are often black and white, with a clear good side and a clear evil side, but the novel's conclusion about humanity is not so simple. On the contrary, Atticus understands that people are capable of great goodness and great evil, which proves the key to his own admirable moral strength. Unlike the children's outlook, Atticus's understanding of the world is not innocent: he does not believe in goodness simply because he has never seen evil. He has indeed seen and experienced evil, but he is nevertheless capable of faith in the good qualities of humankind. This faith represents the adult perspective toward which Scout, who begins the novel as an innocent child, is forced to move as the story progresses. Although the jury strikes a blow for prejudice by convicting Tom, it is still possible for the town's morally unblemished adult characters to hold out hope. Even after the verdict has been handed down, there is a sense that progress has been made: as Miss Maudie puts it, the town has taken "a step—it's just a baby-step, but it's a step."

Jem, however, is not able to see things this way. Scout is bewildered by the verdict, but, like Atticus, she is resilient and retains her positive view of the world. Her brother is crushed: his dearly held illusions about justice and the law have been shattered. In a way, Jem, like Tom Robinson, is a mockingbird. While the Ewells and the forces of hatred and prejudice do not take his life, they do strip him of his childhood and youthful idealism.

CHAPTERS 23–25

SUMMARY: CHAPTER 23

Bob Ewell's threats are worrisome to everyone except Atticus. Atticus tells Jem and Scout that because he made Ewell look like a fool, Ewell needed to get revenge. Now that Ewell has gotten that vengefulness out of his system, Atticus expects no more trouble. Aunt Alexandra and the children remain worried. Meanwhile, Tom Robinson has been sent to another prison seventy miles away while his appeal winds through the court system. Atticus feels that his client has a good chance of being pardoned. When Scout asks what will happen if Tom loses, Atticus replies that Tom will go to the electric chair, as rape is a capital offense in Alabama.

Jem and Atticus discuss the justice of executing men for rape. The subject then turns to jury trials and to how all twelve men could have convicted Tom. Atticus tells Jem that in an Alabama court of law, a white man's word always beats a black man's, and that they were lucky to have the jury out so long. In fact, one man on the jury wanted to acquit—amazingly, it was one of the Cunninghams. Upon hearing this revelation, Scout announces that she wants to invite young Walter Cunningham to dinner, but Aunt Alexandra expressly forbids it, telling her that the Finches do not associate with trash.

Scout grows furious, and Jem hastily takes her out of the room. In his bedroom, Jem reveals his minimal growth of chest hair and tells Scout that he is going to try out for the football team in the fall. They discuss the class system—why their aunt despises the Cunninghams, why the Cunninghams look down on the Ewells, who hate black people, and other such matters. After being unable to figure out why people go out of their way to despise each other, Jem suggests Boo Radley does not come out of his house because he does not want to leave it.

Summary: Chapter 24
One day in August, Aunt Alexandra invites her missionary circle to tea. Scout, wearing a dress, helps Calpurnia bring in the tea, and Alexandra invites Scout to stay with the ladies. Scout listens to the missionary circle first discuss the plight of the poor Mrunas, a benighted African tribe being converted to Christianity, and then talk about how their own black servants have behaved badly ever since Tom Robinson's trial. Miss Maudie shuts up their prattle with icy remarks. Suddenly, Atticus appears and calls Alexandra to the kitchen. There he tells her, Scout, Calpurnia, and Miss Maudie that Tom Robinson attempted to escape and was shot seventeen times. He takes Calpurnia with him to tell the Robinson family of Tom's death. Alexandra asks Miss Maudie how the town can allow Atticus to wreck himself in pursuit of justice. Maudie replies that the town trusts him to do right. They return with Scout to the missionary circle, managing to act as if nothing is wrong.

Summary: Chapter 25
September has begun and Jem and Scout are on the back porch when Scout notices a roly-poly bug. She is about to mash it with

her hand when Jem tells her not to. She dutifully places the bug outside. When she asks Jem why she shouldn't have mashed it, he replies that the bug didn't do anything to harm her. Scout observes that it is Jem, not she, who is becoming more and more like a girl. Her thoughts turn to Dill, and she remembers him telling her that he and Jem ran into Atticus as they started home from swimming during the last two days of August. Jem had convinced Atticus to let them accompany him to Helen Robinson's house, where they saw her collapse even before Atticus could say that her husband, Tom, was dead. Meanwhile, the news occupies Maycomb's attention for about two days, and everyone agrees that it is typical for a black man to do something irrational like try to escape. Mr. Underwood writes a long editorial condemning Tom's death as the murder of an innocent man. The only other significant reaction comes when Bob Ewell is overheard saying that Tom's death makes "one down and about two more to go." Summer ends and Dill leaves.

ANALYSIS: CHAPTERS 23–25

When he reassures his family that Bob Ewell does not really intend to harm him, Atticus advises Jem to stand in Bob Ewell's shoes, echoing the advice that he gives Scout earlier in the novel and evoking one of the most important moral themes in the book. Here, however, Atticus's attempt to understand another human falls short: he makes an honest mistake in his analysis by failing to understand the depth of Ewell's anger toward him. Aunt Alexandra is more insightful, maintaining that a man like Ewell will do anything to get revenge. Although her comments seem typical of her tendency to stereotype "those people" who are different from the Finches, her analysis of Ewell proves correct. For all her faults, Aunt Alexandra gains, by way of her stereotypes, a basically reliable understanding of the people of Maycomb.

Both Jem and Scout are forced to face the adult world in these chapters to an unprecedented degree. In fact, Jem is actually beginning to enter the adult world, showing Scout his chest hair and contemplating trying out for football. Jem and Atticus discuss the judicial system in Maycomb County for much of Chapter 23. Their conversation is an education for Jem in the realities not only of the jury system but also of life. Atticus's revelation that the Cunningham on the jury wanted to acquit Tom presents Jem with a remarkable instance of an uneducated white man being able to see beyond his ingrained racial prejudice—a further indication that the adult world is complex rather than black and white, as is the world of children.

Scout, meanwhile, moves closer to the adult world by drawing closer to Alexandra. Alexandra's refusal to have the lowly Walter Cunningham to dinner puts her at odds with Jem and Scout, providing them with another opportunity to deride Maycomb's ludicrously irrational social hierarchy. But the missionary tea party reveals Alexandra's better side. The scene brilliantly portrays the hypocrisy of the Maycomb ladies. "Mrs. Merriweather's large brown eyes always filled up with tears when she considered the oppressed [in Africa]," Scout notes, yet the same woman can complain that "there's nothing more distracting than a sulky darky." In the wake of hearing of Tom Robinson's tragic death, however, the tea party becomes an opportunity for the Finch women to display moral courage by maintaining a public facade of composure. Mr. Underwood likens Tom's death to "the senseless slaughter of songbirds," an obvious reference to the novel's title. In this moment, Alexandra and Scout stand together as finches, as harmless as mockingbirds, forced to bear the white community's utter disregard of justice.

Whereas Jem embraces entrance into the adult world, Scout seems reluctant about it. Jem proudly shows Scout his chest hair as a mark of his emergence into manhood. Scout's badge of incipient womanhood, the dress that she wears to the missionary circle meeting, doesn't suit her; she wears her usual tomboy trousers underneath. Additionally, whereas Jem intently discusses aspects of the complicated legal system with Atticus, Miss Stephanie teases the young Scout about growing up to be a lawyer. This difference in maturity between Jem and Scout manifests itself in the incident with the roly-poly bug. Wishing to withdraw back into the childhood world of actions without abstract significance, Scout moves to crush the bug. Jem, now sensitive to the vulnerability of those who are oppressed, urges her to leave the defenseless bug alone.

CHAPTERS 26–27

SUMMARY: CHAPTER 26
School starts, and Jem and Scout again begin to pass by the Radley Place every day. They are now too old to be frightened by the house, but Scout still wistfully wishes to see Boo Radley just once. Meanwhile, the shadow of the trial still hangs over her. One day in school, her third-grade teacher, Miss Gates, lectures the class on the

wickedness of Hitler's persecution of the Jews and on the virtues of equality and democracy. Scout listens and later asks Jem how Miss Gates can preach about equality when she came out of the courthouse after the trial and told Miss Stephanie Crawford that it was about time that someone taught the blacks in town a lesson. Jem becomes furious and tells Scout never to mention the trial to him again. Scout, upset, goes to Atticus for comfort.

SUMMARY: CHAPTER 27

By the middle of October, Bob Ewell gets a job with the WPA, one of the Depression job programs, and loses it a few days later. He blames Atticus for "getting" his job. Also in the middle of October, Judge Taylor is home alone and hears someone prowling around; when he goes to investigate, he finds his screen door open and sees a shadow creeping away. Bob Ewell then begins to follow Helen Robinson to work, keeping his distance but whispering obscenities at her. Deas sees Ewell and threatens to have him arrested if he doesn't leave Helen alone; he gives her no further trouble. But these events worry Aunt Alexandra, who points out that Ewell seems to have a grudge against everyone connected with the case.

That Halloween, the town sponsors a party and play at the school. This plan constitutes an attempt to avoid the unsupervised mischief of the previous Halloween, when someone burglarized the house of two elderly sisters and hid all of their furniture in their basement. The play is an "agricultural pageant" in which every child portrays a food: Scout wears a wire mesh shaped to look like ham. Both Atticus and Aunt Alexandra are too tired to attend the festivities, so Jem takes Scout to the school.

ANALYSIS: CHAPTERS 26–27

These short chapters are marked by a mood of mounting mischief laced with a growing sense of real danger. They begin with a reference to the Radley Place, the source of childhood terror that no longer scares Jem and Scout—"Boo Radley was the least of our fears," Scout comments. The dissipation of Jem and Scout's youthful fear of Boo reflects how the trial has hardened them and how, in the wake of the trial's injustice and Bob Ewell's threats, the children have become increasingly mired in the more serious concerns of the adult world. The Radley Place is part of the past now. The aura of scariness attached to the name "Boo" has dissolved into curiosity, perhaps even into fondness. As Jem and Scout gain a greater understanding of Boo, he seems less like a town freak to them and more, in a strange way, like a pet or a plaything. Scout still expresses a wish to see Boo someday, and she remembers fondly the near encounters with Boo during summers past. These memories restore Boo Radley to the reader's consciousness, which has been occupied with the trial for most of Part Two, thereby foreshadowing Boo's appearance a few chapters later.

Meanwhile, the aftereffects of the trial continue to loom, and Jem and Scout's fading fear of Boo accentuates the real danger that Bob Ewell's various attempts at revenge present. Bob Ewell shows himself to be sinister, and the fact that he has not yet attempted anything against the Finches only increases the sense of foreboding. Atticus remains confident in his own safety, but this confidence begins to seem like wishful thinking. In fact, rather than offer further thematic commentary, Lee devotes a great part of these chapters to building tension and suspense by focusing on the unpredictable threat that Bob Ewell poses. The misdeeds of the previous Halloween, which lead to the idea of a Halloween play this year, hint again at the damage caused by those who act without conscience.

Meanwhile, the incident involving Miss Gates reveals the extent to which Jem remains affected by the trial. Despite the grim experience of the trial, Scout retains her faith in the basic goodness of others, and thus her teacher's obvious hypocrisy confuses her. Jem, meanwhile, has become disillusioned, and when Scout tries to talk to him about Miss Gates, he shuts himself off from the painful memory of the trial. Bob Ewell's threats are not the only dark cloud hanging over the Finch household in this section: the injustice of the trial has changed Jem irrevocably.

Chapters 28–31

Summary: Chapter 28

It is dark on the way to the school, and Cecil Jacobs jumps out and frightens Jem and Scout. Scout and Cecil wander around the crowded school, visiting the haunted house in a seventh-grade classroom and buying homemade candy. The pageant nears its start and all of the children go backstage. Scout, however, has fallen asleep and consequently misses her entrance. She runs onstage at the end, prompting Judge Taylor and many others to burst out laughing. The woman in charge of the pageant accuses Scout of ruining it. Scout is so ashamed that she and Jem wait backstage until the crowd is gone before they make their way home.

On the walk back home, Jem hears noises behind him and Scout. They think it must be Cecil Jacobs trying to frighten them again, but when they call out to him, they hear no reply. They have almost reached the road when their pursuer begins running after them. Jem screams for Scout to run, but in the dark, hampered by her costume, she loses her balance and falls. Something tears at the metal mesh, and she hears struggling behind her. Jem then breaks free and drags Scout almost all the way to the road before their assailant pulls him back. Scout hears a crunching sound and Jem screams; she runs toward him and is grabbed and squeezed. Suddenly, her attacker is pulled away. Once the noise of struggling has ceased, Scout feels on the ground for Jem, finding only the prone figure of an unshaven man smelling of whiskey. She stumbles toward home, and sees, in the light of the streetlamp, a man carrying Jem toward her house.

Scout reaches home, and Aunt Alexandra goes to call Dr. Reynolds. Atticus calls Heck Tate, telling him that someone has attacked his children. Alexandra removes Scout's costume, and tells her that Jem is only unconscious, not dead. Dr. Reynolds then arrives and goes into Jem's room. When he emerges, he informs Scout that Jem has a broken arm and a bump on his head, but that he will be all right. Scout goes in to see Jem. The man who carried him home is in the room, but she does not recognize him. Heck Tate appears and tells Atticus that Bob Ewell is lying under a tree, dead, with a knife stuck under his ribs.

SUMMARY: CHAPTER 29
As Scout tells everyone what she heard and saw, Heck Tate shows her costume with a mark on it where a knife slashed and was stopped by the wire. When Scout gets to the point in the story where Jem was picked up and carried home, she turns to the man in the corner and really looks at him for the first time. He is pale, with torn clothes and a thin, pinched face and colorless eyes. She realizes that it is Boo Radley.

SUMMARY: CHAPTER 30
Scout takes Boo—"Mr. Arthur"—down to the porch, and they sit in shadow listening to Atticus and Heck Tate argue. Heck insists on calling the death an accident, but Atticus, thinking that Jem killed Bob Ewell, doesn't want his son protected from the law. Heck corrects him—Ewell fell on his knife; Jem didn't kill him. Although he

knows that Boo is the one who stabbed Ewell, Heck wants to hush up the whole affair, saying that Boo doesn't need the attention of the neighborhood brought to his door. Tom Robinson died for no reason, he says, and now the man responsible is dead: "Let the dead bury the dead."

SUMMARY: CHAPTER 31

> *Atticus was right. One time he said you never really know a man until you stand in his shoes and walk around in them. Just standing on the Radley porch was enough.*
>
> (See QUOTATIONS, p. 58)

Scout takes Boo upstairs to say goodnight to Jem and then walks him home. He goes inside his house, and she never sees him again. But, for just a moment, she imagines the world from his perspective. She returns home and finds Atticus sitting in Jem's room. He reads one of Jem's books to her until she falls asleep.

> *"When they finally saw him, why he hadn't done any of those things . . . Atticus, he was real nice. . . ."*
> *"Most people are, Scout, when you finally see them."*
>
> (See QUOTATIONS, p. 59)

ANALYSIS: CHAPTERS 28–31

Lee fills the night of the pageant with elements of foreshadowing, from the sense of foreboding that grips Aunt Alexandra just before Jem and Scout leave the house, to the ominous, pitch-dark night to Cecil Jacobs's attempt to scare them. The pageant itself is an amusing depiction of small-town pride, as the lady in charge spends thirty minutes describing the exploits of Colonel Maycomb, the town's founder, to the audience. Additionally, the reader can visualize the comical parade of meats and vegetables crossing the stage, with Scout, just awake, hurrying after them as the audience roars with laughter. In this way, as with the early snowfall, the fire, and the mad dog, the night of the pageant incorporates both the Gothic motif of the novel and the motif of small-town life that counterbalances it.

A mood of mounting suspense marks Jem and Scout's walk home. They hear the noise of their pursuer and assume it to be Cecil Jacobs, only to realize relatively quickly that they are in mortal danger. The attack is all the more terrifying because Jem and Scout are vulnerable: they are very near their home, in an area that they assume to be safe, and Scout, in her awkward costume, has no idea what is happening. Though Lee has spent a great deal of time fore-shadowing Ewell's impending attack on the Finches, she manages to make the scene of the attack surprising. All of the clues in the novel to this point have suggested that Ewell would attack Atticus, not the children. But, as we realize in this scene, the cowardly Ewell would never have the courage to attack the best shot in Maycomb County; his insidious, malicious attack on the children reveals how loathsome a man he is. In this way, Lee's diversionary technique of leading the reader to suspect that Atticus would be Ewell's victim makes this scene simultaneously startling for the reader and reveal-ing of character.

Boo Radley's entrance takes place in the thick of the scuffle, and Scout does not realize that her reclusive neighbor has saved them until she has reached home; even then, she assumes him to be "some countryman." This failure of recognition symbolizes the inability of Scout and the other children, throughout the novel, to see Boo as a human being, treating him instead as merely a source of childhood ghost stories. As his name suggests, Boo is a sort of ghost, but this condition has less to do with his appearance out of nowhere on Halloween than with Scout's hollow understanding of him. When Scout finally realizes who has saved her, however, Boo the child-hood phantom becomes Boo the human being: "His lips parted into a timid smile, and our neighbor's image blurred with my sudden tears. 'Hey, Boo,' I said." With this sentence, Scout takes the first of two large steps in this section toward completing the development of her character and assuming the grown-up moral perspective that Atticus has shown her throughout the book.

Heck Tate's decision to spare Boo the horror of publicity by say-ing that Bob Ewell fell on his knife invokes the title of the book and its central theme one last time, as Scout says that exposing Boo to the public eye would be "sort of like shootin' a mockingbird." She has appropriated not only Atticus's words but also his outlook, as she suddenly sees the world through Boo's eyes. In this moment of understanding and sympathy, Scout takes her second great step toward a grown-up moral perspective. The reader gets the sense that all of Scout's previous experiences have led her to this enriching moment and that Scout will be able to grow up without having her experience of evil destroy her faith in goodness. Not only has Boo become a real person to her, but in saving the children's lives he has also provided concrete proof that goodness exists in powerful and unexpected forms, just as evil does.

Despite Scout's obvious maturation in Chapter 31, the novel closes with her falling asleep as Atticus reads to her. This enduring image of her as Atticus's baby child is fitting—while she has grown up quite a bit over the course of the novel, she is still, after all, only eight years old. Just as her ham costume, a symbol of the silly and carefree nature of childhood, prevents Bob Ewell's knife from injuring her, so does the timely intervention of Boo, another part of Scout's childhood, thwart the total intrusion into her life of the often hate-filled adult world that Ewell represents. Interestingly, the book makes no return to the adult Scout for closing narration, and Lee offers the reader no details of Scout's future except that she never sees Boo again. Rather, she leaves Scout and the reader with a powerful feeling of cautious optimism—an acknowledgment that the existence of evil is balanced by faith in the essential goodness of humankind.

SUMMARY & ANALYSIS

IMPORTANT QUOTATIONS EXPLAINED

1. Maycomb was an old town, but it was a tired old town
    when I first knew it. In rainy weather the streets turned to
    red slop . . . [s]omehow it was hotter then . . . bony mules
    hitched to Hoover carts flicked flies in the sweltering shade
    of the live oaks on the square. Men's stiff collars wilted by
    nine in the morning. Ladies bathed before noon, after their
    three-o'clock naps, and by nightfall were like soft teacakes
    with frostings of sweat and sweet talcum. . . . There was no
    hurry, for there was nowhere to go, nothing to buy and no
    money to buy it with, nothing to see outside the boundaries
    of Maycomb County. But it was a time of vague optimism
    for some of the people: Maycomb County had recently
    been told that it had nothing to fear but fear itself.

This quotation, from Chapter 1, is Scout's introductory description of
Maycomb. Scout emphasizes the slow pace, Alabama heat, and old-
fashioned values of the town, in which men wear shirt collars, ladies
use talcum powder, and the streets are not paved, turning to "red slop"
in the rain. This description situates Maycomb in the reader's mind
as a sleepy Southern town; Scout even calls it "tired." It also situates
Scout with respect to the narrative: she writes of the time when she
"first knew" Maycomb, indicating that she embarks upon this recollection of her childhood much later in life, as an adult. The description
also provides important clues about the story's chronological setting: in
addition to now-outdated elements such as mule-driven Hoover carts
and dirt roads, it also makes reference to the widespread poverty of the
town, implying that Maycomb is in the midst of the Great Depression.

   "We have nothing to fear but fear itself" is the most famous line
from Franklin Delano Roosevelt's first inaugural speech, made after
the 1932 presidential election. From this clue, it is reasonable to
infer that the action of the story opens in the summer of 1933, an
assumption that subsequent historical clues support. The defeat
of the National Recovery Act in the Supreme Court in 1935, for
instance, is mentioned in Chapter 27 of the novel, when Scout is
eight—about two years older than at the start of the novel.

2.   You never really understand a person until you consider things from his point of view . . . until you climb into his skin and walk around in it.

This important snippet of conversation from Chapter 3 finds Atticus giving Scout the crucial piece of moral advice that governs her development for the rest of the novel. The simple wisdom of Atticus's words reflects the uncomplicated manner in which he guides himself by this sole principle. His ability to relate to his children is manifested in his restatement of this principle in terms that Scout can understand ("climb into his skin and walk around in it"). Scout struggles, with varying degrees of success, to put Atticus's advice into practice and to live with sympathy and understanding toward others. At the end of the book, she succeeds in comprehending Boo Radley's perspective, fulfilling Atticus's advice in Chapter 3 and providing the novel with an optimistic ending despite the considerable darkness of the plot.

3. "Remember it's a sin to kill a mockingbird." That was
    the only time I ever heard Atticus say it was a sin to do
    something, and I asked Miss Maudie about it.
    "Your father's right," she said. "Mockingbirds don't
    do one thing but make music for us to enjoy . . . but
    sing their hearts out for us. That's why it's a sin to kill a
    mockingbird."

These lines from Chapter 10 are the source of the novel's title and introduce one of the key metaphors of the book: the idea of "mockingbirds" as good, innocent people who are destroyed by evil. Boo Radley, for instance, is like a mockingbird—just as mockingbirds do not harm people but only "sing their hearts out for us," Boo does not harm anyone; instead, he leaves Jem and Scout presents, covers Scout with a blanket during the fire, and eventually saves the children from Bob Ewell. Despite the pureness of his heart, however, Boo has been damaged by an abusive father. The connection between songbirds and innocents is made explicitly several times in the book: in Chapter 25, Mr. Underwood likens Tom Robinson's death to "the senseless slaughter of songbirds by hunters and children"; in Chapter 30, Scout tells Atticus that hurting Boo Radley would be "sort of like shootin' a mockingbird." The moral imperative to protect the vulnerable governs Atticus's decision to take Tom's case, just as it leads Jem to protect the roly-poly bug from Scout's hand.

4. A boy trudged down the sidewalk dragging a fishing pole
    behind him. A man stood waiting with his hands on his
    hips. Summertime, and his children played in the front
    yard with their friend, enacting a strange little drama of
    their own invention. It was fall, and his children fought
    on the sidewalk in front of Mrs. Dubose's. . . . Fall, and
    his children trotted to and fro around the corner, the day's
    woes and triumphs on their faces. They stopped at an oak
    tree, delighted, puzzled, apprehensive. Winter, and his
    children shivered at the front gate, silhouetted against a
    blazing house. Winter, and a man walked into the street,
    dropped his glasses, and shot a dog. Summer, and he
    watched his children's heart break. Autumn again, and
    Boo's children needed him. Atticus was right. One time
    he said you never really know a man until you stand in
    his shoes and walk around in them. Just standing on the
    Radley porch was enough.

This passage from Chapter 31 is Scout's exercise in thinking about
the world from Boo Radley's perspective. After she walks him home,
Scout stands on Boo's porch and imagines many of the events of
the story (Atticus shooting the mad dog, the children finding Boo's
presents in the oak tree) as they must have looked to Boo. She at last
realizes the love and protection that he has silently offered her and
Jem all along. The blossoming of Scout's ability to assume another
person's perspective sympathetically is the culmination of her novel-
long development as a character and of *To Kill a Mockingbird*'s
moral outlook as a whole.

5.   "When they finally saw him, why he hadn't done any of
those things . . . Atticus, he was real nice. . . ." His hands
were under my chin, pulling up the cover, tucking it around
me. "Most people are, Scout, when you finally see them."
He turned out the light and went into Jem's room. He
would be there all night, and he would be there when Jem
waked up in the morning.

These words, from Chapter 31, conclude the novel. As Scout falls
asleep, she is telling Atticus about the events of *The Gray Ghost,*
a book in which one of the characters is wrongly accused of com-
mitting a crime and is pursued. When he is finally caught, however,
his innocence is revealed. As Scout sleepily explains the story to
Atticus, saying that the character was "real nice" when "they finally
saw him," Atticus gently notes the truth of that observation. In this
way, Lee closes the book with a subtle reminder of the themes of innocence, accusation, and threat that have run throughout it, putting
them to rest by again illustrating the wise moral outlook of Atticus:
if one lives with sympathy and understanding, then it is possible to
retain faith in humanity despite its capacity for evil—to believe that
most people are "real nice." Additionally, this passage emphasizes
Atticus's strong, loving role as a parent to Scout and Jem—he tucks
Scout in, then goes to sit by Jem's bedside all night long. Through
Atticus's strength, the tension and danger of the previous chapters
are resolved, and the book ends on a note of security and peace.

QUOTATIONS

Key Facts

FULL TITLE
To Kill a Mockingbird

AUTHOR
Harper Lee

TYPE OF WORK
Novel

GENRE
Coming-of-age story; social drama; courtroom drama; Southern drama

LANGUAGE
English

TIME AND PLACE WRITTEN
Mid-1950s; New York City

DATE OF FIRST PUBLICATION
1960

PUBLISHER
J. B. Lippincott

NARRATOR
Scout narrates the story herself, looking back in retrospect an unspecified number of years after the events of the novel take place.

POINT OF VIEW
Scout narrates in the first person, telling what she saw and heard at the time and augmenting this narration with thoughts and assessments of her experiences in retrospect. Although she is by no means an omniscient narrator, she has matured considerably over the intervening years and often implicitly and humorously comments on the naïveté she displayed in her thoughts and actions as a young girl. Scout mostly tells of her own thoughts but also devotes considerable time to recounting and analyzing Jem's thoughts and actions.

TONE

Childlike, humorous, nostalgic, innocent; as the novel progresses, increasingly dark, foreboding, and critical of society

TENSE

Past

SETTING (TIME)

1933–1935

SETTING (PLACE)

The fictional town of Maycomb, Alabama

PROTAGONIST

Scout Finch

MAJOR CONFLICT

The childhood innocence with which Scout and Jem begin the novel is threatened by numerous incidents that expose the evil side of human nature, most notably the guilty verdict in Tom Robinson's trial and the vengefulness of Bob Ewell. As the novel progresses, Scout and Jem struggle to maintain faith in the human capacity for good in light of these recurring instances of human evil.

RISING ACTION

Scout, Jem, and Dill become fascinated with their mysterious neighbor Boo Radley and have an escalating series of encounters with him. Meanwhile, Atticus is assigned to defend a black man, Tom Robinson against the spurious rape charges Bob Ewell has brought against him. Watching the trial, Scout, and especially Jem, cannot understand how a jury could possibly convict Tom Robinson based on the Ewells' clearly fabricated story.

CLIMAX

Despite Atticus's capable and impassioned defense, the jury finds Tom Robinson guilty. The verdict forces Scout and Jem to confront the fact that the morals Atticus has taught them cannot always be reconciled with the reality of the world and the evils of human nature.

FALLING ACTION

When word spreads that Tom Robinson has been shot while trying to escape from prison, Jem struggles to come to terms with the injustice of the trial and of Tom Robinson's fate.

After making a variety of threats against Atticus and others connected with the trial, Bob Ewell assaults Scout and Jem as they walk home one night, but Boo Radley saves the children and fatally stabs Ewell. The sheriff, knowing that Boo, like Tom Robinson, would be misunderstood and likely convicted in a trial, protects Boo by saying that Ewell tripped and fell on his own knife. After sitting and talking with Scout briefly, Boo retreats into his house, and Scout never sees him again.

THEMES

The coexistence of good and evil; the importance of moral education; social class

MOTIFS

Gothic details; small-town life

SYMBOLS

Mockingbirds; Boo Radley

FORESHADOWING

The Gothic elements of the novel (the fire, the mad dog) build tension that subtly foreshadows Tom Robinson's trial and tragic death; Burris Ewell's appearance in school foreshadows the nastiness of Bob Ewell; the presents Jem and Scout find in the oak tree foreshadow the eventual discovery of Boo Radley's good-heartedness; Bob Ewell's threats and suspicious behavior after the trial foreshadow his attack on the children.

STUDY QUESTIONS

1. *Discuss Atticus's parenting style. What is his relationship to his children like? How does he seek to instill conscience in them?*

Atticus is a wise man, committed to justice and equality, and his parenting style is based on fostering these virtues in his children—he even encourages Jem and Scout to call him "Atticus" so that they can interact on terms as equal as possible. Throughout the novel, Atticus works to develop Scout's and Jem's respective consciences, through both teaching, as when he tells Scout to put herself in a person's shoes before she judges them, and example, as when he takes Tom Robinson's case, living up to his own moral standards despite the harsh consequences he knows he will face. Atticus is a kind and loving father, reading to his children and offering them comfort when they need it, but he is also capable of teaching them harsh lessons, as when he allows Jem to come with him to tell Helen Robinson about Tom's death. At the end of the novel, when Atticus believes that Jem killed Bob Ewell, he tries to talk Heck Tate, the sheriff, out of calling the death an accident—Atticus's standards are firm, and he does not want his son to have unfair protection from the law.

2. *Analyze the trial scene and its relationship to the rest of the novel.*

To Kill a Mockingbird explores the questions of innocence and harsh experience, good and evil, from several different angles. Tom Robinson's trial explores these ideas by examining the evil of racial prejudice, its ability to poison an otherwise admirable Southern town and destroy an innocent man, and its effect on young Jem and Scout. Because the point of a trial is to discover guilt or innocence, Tom's trial serves as a useful mechanism for Lee to lay out the argument against racial prejudice in a dramatic framework suited to the larger themes of the novel. Additionally, because a trial is essentially about the presentation of facts, it serves as a laboratory in which the extent of the town's prejudice can be objectively measured. Atticus presents a solid case that leaves virtually no room for doubt: Tom Robinson is innocent, and if he is found guilty, then it is only because of the jury's racism. When Tom is found guilty, the outcome of the trial presents a crisis of confidence, particularly for Jem: if the law fails, then how can one have faith in justice, and if the people of Maycomb fail, then how can one have faith in the goodness of humanity? Although these questions are explored to some degree before the trial, they dominate the novel after the trial. From a structural point of view, the trial serves to bring the narrative's main issues into focus.

3. *Discuss the author's portrayal of the black community and the characters of Calpurnia and Tom Robinson. Are they realistic or idealized?*

The black community in Maycomb is quite idealized, especially in the scenes at the black church and in the "colored balcony" during the trial. Lee's portrayal of the black community isn't unrealistic or unbelievable; it is important to point out, however, that she emphasizes all of the good qualities of the community without ever pointing out any of the bad ones. The black community is shown to be loving, affectionate, welcoming, pious, honest, hardworking, close-knit, and forthright. Calpurnia and Tom, members of this community, possess remarkable dignity and moral courage. But the idealization of the black community serves an important purpose in the novel, heightening the contrast between victims and victimizers. The town's black citizens are the novel's victims, oppressed by white prejudice and forced to live in an environment where the mere word of a man like Bob Ewell can doom them to life in prison, or even execution, with no other evidence. By presenting the blacks of Maycomb as virtuous victims—good people made to suffer—Lee makes her moral condemnation of prejudice direct, emphatic, and explicit.

How to Write
Literary Analysis

The Literary Essay: A Step-by-Step Guide

When you read for pleasure, your only goal is enjoyment. You might find yourself reading to get caught up in an exciting story, to learn about an interesting time or place, or just to pass time. Maybe you're looking for inspiration, guidance, or a reflection of your own life. There are as many different, valid ways of reading a book as there are books in the world.

When you read a work of literature in an English class, however, you're being asked to read in a special way: you're being asked to perform *literary analysis*. To analyze something means to break it down into smaller parts and then examine how those parts work, both individually and together. Literary analysis involves examining all the parts of a novel, play, short story, or poem—elements such as character, setting, tone, and imagery—and thinking about how the author uses those elements to create certain effects.

A literary essay isn't a book review: you're not being asked whether or not you liked a book or whether you'd recommend it to another reader. A literary essay also isn't like the kind of book report you wrote when you were younger, where your teacher wanted you to summarize the book's action. A high school- or college-level literary essay asks, "How does this piece of literature actually work?" "How does it do what it does?" and, "Why might the author have made the choices he or she did?"

The Seven Steps
No one is born knowing how to analyze literature; it's a skill you learn and a process you can master. As you gain more practice with this kind of thinking and writing, you'll be able to craft a method that works best for you. But until then, here are seven basic steps to writing a well-constructed literary essay:

1. *Ask questions*
2. *Collect evidence*
3. *Construct a thesis*

4. Develop and organize arguments
5. Write the introduction
6. Write the body paragraphs
7. Write the conclusion

---

1. ASK QUESTIONS

When you're assigned a literary essay in class, your teacher will often provide you with a list of writing prompts. Lucky you! Now all you have to do is choose one. Do yourself a favor and pick a topic that interests you. You'll have a much better (not to mention easier) time if you start off with something you enjoy thinking about. If you are asked to come up with a topic by yourself, though, you might start to feel a little panicked. Maybe you have too many ideas—or none at all. Don't worry. Take a deep breath and start by asking yourself these questions:

- **What struck you?** Did a particular image, line, or scene linger in your mind for a long time? If it fascinated you, chances are you can draw on it to write a fascinating essay.

- **What confused you?** Maybe you were surprised to see a character act in a certain way, or maybe you didn't understand why the book ended the way it did. Confusing moments in a work of literature are like a loose thread in a sweater: if you pull on it, you can unravel the entire thing. Ask yourself why the author chose to write about that character or scene the way he or she did and you might tap into some important insights about the work as a whole.

- **Did you notice any patterns?** Is there a phrase that the main character uses constantly or an image that repeats throughout the book? If you can figure out how that pattern weaves through the work and what the significance of that pattern is, you've almost got your entire essay mapped out.

- **Did you notice any contradictions or ironies?** Great works of literature are complex; great literary essays recognize and explain those complexities. Maybe the title (*Happy Days*) totally disagrees with the book's subject matter (hungry orphans dying in the woods). Maybe the main character acts one way around his family and a completely different way around his friends and associates. If you can find a way to explain a work's contradictory elements, you've got the seeds of a great essay.

At this point, you don't need to know exactly what you're going to say about your topic; you just need a place to begin your exploration. You can help direct your reading and brainstorming by formulating your topic as a *question,* which you'll then try to answer in your essay. The best questions invite critical debates and discussions, not just a rehashing of the summary. Remember, you're looking for something you can *prove or argue* based on evidence you find in the text. Finally, remember to keep the scope of your question in mind: is this a topic you can adequately address within the word or page limit you've been given? Conversely, is this a topic big enough to fill the required length?

GOOD QUESTIONS

"Are Romeo and Juliet's parents responsible for the deaths of their children?"

"Why do pigs keep showing up in LORD OF THE FLIES*?"*

"Are Dr. Frankenstein and his monster alike? How?"

BAD QUESTIONS

"What happens to Scout in TO KILL A MOCKINGBIRD*?"*

"What do the other characters in JULIUS CAESAR *think about Caesar?"*

"How does Hester Prynne in THE SCARLET LETTER *remind me of my sister?"*

2. COLLECT EVIDENCE

Once you know what question you want to answer, it's time to scour the book for things that will help you answer the question. Don't worry if you don't know what you want to say yet—right now you're just collecting ideas and material and letting it all percolate. Keep track of passages, symbols, images, or scenes that deal with your topic. Eventually, you'll start making connections between these examples and your thesis will emerge.

Here's a brief summary of the various parts that compose each and every work of literature. These are the elements that you will analyze in your essay, and which you will offer as evidence to support your arguments. For more on the parts of literary works, see the Glossary of Literary Terms at the end of this section.

ELEMENTS OF STORY   These are the *what*s of the work—what happens, where it happens, and to whom it happens.

- **Plot:** All of the events and actions of the work.
- **Character:** The people who act and are acted upon in a literary work. The main character of a work is known as the *protagonist.*
- **Conflict:** The central tension in the work. In most cases, the protagonist wants something, while opposing forces (antagonists) hinder the protagonist's progress.
- **Setting:** When and where the work takes place. Elements of setting include location, time period, time of day, weather, social atmosphere, and economic conditions.
- **Narrator:** The person telling the story. The narrator may straightforwardly report what happens, convey the subjective opinions and perceptions of one or more characters, or provide commentary and opinion in his or her own voice.
- **Themes:** The main idea or message of the work—usually an abstract idea about people, society, or life in general. A work may have many themes, which may be in tension with one another.

ELEMENTS OF STYLE   These are the *how*s—how the characters speak, how the story is constructed, and how language is used throughout the work.

- **Structure and organization:** How the parts of the work are assembled. Some novels are narrated in a linear, chronological fashion, while others skip around in time. Some plays follow a traditional three- or five-act structure, while others are a series of loosely connected scenes. Some authors deliberately leave gaps in their works, leaving readers to puzzle out the missing information. A work's structure and organization can tell you a lot about the kind of message it wants to convey.
- **Point of view:** The perspective from which a story is told. In *first-person point of view,* the narrator involves him or herself in the story. ("I went to the store"; "We watched in horror as the bird slammed into the window.") A first-person narrator is usually the protagonist of the work, but not always. In *third-person point of view,* the narrator does not participate

in the story. A third-person narrator may closely follow a specific character, recounting that individual character's thoughts or experiences, or it may be what we call an *omniscient* narrator. Omniscient narrators see and know all: they can witness any event in any time or place and are privy to the inner thoughts and feelings of all characters. Remember that the narrator and the author are not the same thing!

- **Diction:** Word choice. Whether a character uses dry, clinical language or flowery prose with lots of exclamation points can tell you a lot about his or her attitude and personality.

- **Syntax:** Word order and sentence construction. Syntax is a crucial part of establishing an author's narrative voice. Ernest Hemingway, for example, is known for writing in very short, straightforward sentences, while James Joyce characteristically wrote in long, incredibly complicated lines.

- **Tone:** The mood or feeling of the text. Diction and syntax often contribute to the tone of a work. A novel written in short, clipped sentences that use small, simple words might feel brusque, cold, or matter-of-fact.

- **Imagery:** Language that appeals to the senses, representing things that can be seen, smelled, heard, tasted, or touched.

- **Figurative language:** Language that is not meant to be interpreted literally. The most common types of figurative language are *metaphors* and *similes,* which compare two unlike things in order to suggest a similarity between them— for example, "All the world's a stage," or "The moon is like a ball of green cheese." (Metaphors say one thing *is* another thing; similes claim that one thing is *like* another thing.)

---

3. CONSTRUCT A THESIS

When you've examined all the evidence you've collected and know how you want to answer the question, it's time to write your thesis statement. A *thesis* is a claim about a work of literature that needs to be supported by evidence and arguments. The thesis statement is the heart of the literary essay, and the bulk of your paper will be spent trying to prove this claim. A good thesis will be:

- **Arguable.** "*The Great Gatsby* describes New York society in the 1920s" isn't a thesis—it's a fact.

LITERARY ANALYSIS

- **Provable through textual evidence**. "*Hamlet* is a confusing but ultimately very well-written play" is a weak thesis because it offers the writer's personal opinion about the book. Yes, it's arguable, but it's not a claim that can be proved or supported with examples taken from the play itself.

- **Surprising**. "Both George and Lenny change a great deal in *Of Mice and Men*" is a weak thesis because it's obvious. A really strong thesis will argue for a reading of the text that is not immediately apparent.

- **Specific**. "Dr. Frankenstein's monster tells us a lot about the human condition" is *almost* a really great thesis statement, but it's still too vague. What does the writer mean by "a lot"? *How* does the monster tell us so much about the human condition?

GOOD THESIS STATEMENTS

Question: In *Romeo and Juliet*, which is more powerful in shaping the lovers' story: fate or foolishness?

Thesis: "Though Shakespeare defines Romeo and Juliet as 'star-crossed lovers' and images of stars and planets appear throughout the play, a closer examination of that celestial imagery reveals that the stars are merely witnesses to the characters' foolish activities and not the causes themselves."

Question: How does the bell jar function as a symbol in Sylvia Plath's *The Bell Jar*?

Thesis: "A bell jar is a bell-shaped glass that has three basic uses: to hold a specimen for observation, to contain gases, and to maintain a vacuum. The bell jar appears in each of these capacities in *The Bell Jar*, Plath's semi-autobiographical novel, and each appearances marks a different stage in Esther's mental breakdown."

Question: Would Piggy in *The Lord of the Flies* make a good island leader if he were given the chance?

Thesis: "Though the intelligent, rational, and innovative Piggy has the mental characteristics of a good leader, he ultimately lacks the social skills necessary to be an effective one. Golding emphasizes this point by giving Piggy a foil in the charismatic Jack, whose magnetic personality allows him to capture and wield power effectively, if not always wisely."

4. DEVELOP AND ORGANIZE ARGUMENTS

The reasons and examples that support your thesis will form the middle paragraphs of your essay. Since you can't really write your thesis statement until you know how you'll structure your argument, you'll probably end up working on steps 3 and 4 at the same time.

There's no single method of argumentation that will work in every context. One essay prompt might ask you to compare and contrast two characters, while another asks you to trace an image through a given work of literature. These questions require different kinds of answers and therefore different kinds of arguments. Below, we'll discuss three common kinds of essay prompts and some strategies for constructing a solid, well-argued case.

TYPES OF LITERARY ESSAYS

- **Compare and contrast**

  Compare and contrast the characters of Huck and Jim in THE ADVENTURES OF HUCKLEBERRY FINN.

  Chances are you've written this kind of essay before. In an academic literary context, you'll organize your arguments the same way you would in any other class. You can either go *subject by subject* or *point by point*. In the former, you'll discuss one character first and then the second. In the latter, you'll choose several traits (attitude toward life, social status, images and metaphors associated with the character) and devote a paragraph to each. You may want to use a mix of these two approaches—for example, you may want to spend a paragraph a piece broadly sketching Huck's and Jim's personalities before transitioning into a paragraph or two that describes a few key points of comparison. This can be a highly effective strategy if you want to make a counterintuitive argument—that, despite seeming to be totally different, the two objects being compared are actually similar in a very important way (or vice versa). Remember that your essay should reveal something fresh or unexpected about the text, so think beyond the obvious parallels and differences.

- **Trace**

  Choose an image—for example, birds, knives, or eyes—and trace that image throughout MACBETH.

  Sounds pretty easy, right? All you need to do is read the play, underline every appearance of a knife in *Macbeth,* and then list them in your essay in the order they appear, right? Well, not exactly. Your teacher doesn't want a simple catalog of examples. He or she wants to see you make *connections* between those examples—that's the difference between summarizing and analyzing. In the *Macbeth* example above, think about the different contexts in which knives appear in the play and to what effect. In *Macbeth*, there are real knives and imagined knives; knives that kill and knives that simply threaten. Categorize and classify your examples to give them some order. Finally, always keep the overall effect in mind. After you choose and analyze your examples, you should come to some greater understanding about the work, as well as your chosen image, symbol, or phrase's role in developing the major themes and stylistic strategies of that work.

- **Debate**

  Is the society depicted in 1984 good for its citizens?

  In this kind of essay, you're being asked to debate a moral, ethical, or aesthetic issue regarding the work. You might be asked to judge a character or group of characters (*Is Caesar responsible for his own demise?*) or the work itself (*Is* JANE EYRE *a feminist novel?*). For this kind of essay, there are two important points to keep in mind. First, don't simply base your arguments on your personal feelings and reactions. Every literary essay expects you to read and analyze the work, so search for evidence in the text. What do characters in *1984* have to say about the government of Oceania? What images does Orwell use that might give you a hint about his attitude toward the government? As in any debate, you also need to make sure that you define all the necessary terms before you begin to argue your case. What does it mean to be a "good" society? What makes a novel "feminist"? You should define your terms right up front, in the first paragraph after your introduction.

  Second, remember that strong literary essays make contrary and surprising arguments. Try to think outside the box. In the *1984* example above, it seems like the obvious answer would be no, the totalitarian society depicted in Orwell's novel is *not* good for its citizens. But can you think of any arguments for the opposite side? Even if your final assertion is that the novel depicts a cruel, repressive, and therefore harmful society, acknowledging and responding to the counterargument will strengthen your overall case.

5. WRITE THE INTRODUCTION

Your introduction sets up the entire essay. It's where you present your topic and articulate the particular issues and questions you'll be addressing. It's also where you, as the writer, introduce yourself to your readers. A persuasive literary essay immediately establishes its writer as a knowledgeable, authoritative figure.

An introduction can vary in length depending on the overall length of the essay, but in a traditional five-paragraph essay it should be no longer than one paragraph. However long it is, your introduction needs to:

- **Provide any necessary context.** Your introduction should situate the reader and let him or her know what to expect. What book are you discussing? Which characters? What topic will you be addressing?

- **Answer the "So what?" question.** Why is this topic important, and why is your particular position on the topic noteworthy? Ideally, your introduction should pique the reader's interest by suggesting how your argument is surprising or otherwise counterintuitive. Literary essays make unexpected connections and reveal less-than-obvious truths.

- **Present your thesis.** This usually happens at or very near the end of your introduction.

- **Indicate the shape of the essay to come.** Your reader should finish reading your introduction with a good sense of the scope of your essay as well as the path you'll take toward proving your thesis. You don't need to spell out every step, but you do need to suggest the organizational pattern you'll be using.

Your introduction should not:

- **Be vague.** Beware of the two killer words in literary analysis: *interesting* and *important*. Of course the work, question, or example is interesting and important—that's why you're writing about it!

- **Open with any grandiose assertions.** Many student readers think that beginning their essays with a flamboyant statement such as, "Since the dawn of time, writers have been fascinated with the topic of free will," makes them sound important and commanding. You know what? It actually sounds pretty amateurish.

- **Wildly praise the work.** Another typical mistake student writers make is extolling the work or author. Your teacher doesn't need to be told that "Shakespeare is perhaps the greatest writer in the English language." You can mention a work's reputation in passing—by referring to *The Adventures of Huckleberry Finn* as "Mark Twain's enduring classic," for example—but don't make a point of bringing it up unless that reputation is key to your argument.

- **Go off-topic.** Keep your introduction streamlined and to the point. Don't feel the need to throw in all kinds of bells and whistles in order to impress your reader—just get to the point as quickly as you can, without skimping on any of the required steps.

6. WRITE THE BODY PARAGRAPHS

Once you've written your introduction, you'll take the arguments you developed in step 4 and turn them into your body paragraphs. The organization of this middle section of your essay will largely be determined by the argumentative strategy you use, but no matter how you arrange your thoughts, your body paragraphs need to do the following:

- **Begin with a strong topic sentence.** Topic sentences are like signs on a highway: they tell the reader where they are and where they're going. A good topic sentence not only alerts readers to what issue will be discussed in the following paragraph but also gives them a sense of what argument will be made *about* that issue. "Rumor and gossip play an important role in *The Crucible*" isn't a strong topic sentence because it doesn't tell us very much. "The community's constant gossiping creates an environment that allows false accusations to flourish" is a much stronger topic sentence— it not only tells us *what* the paragraph will discuss (gossip) but *how* the paragraph will discuss the topic (by showing how gossip creates a set of conditions that leads to the play's climactic action).

- **Fully and completely develop a single thought.** Don't skip around in your paragraph or try to stuff in too much material. Body paragraphs are like bricks: each individual

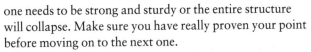

one needs to be strong and sturdy or the entire structure will collapse. Make sure you have really proven your point before moving on to the next one.

- **Use transitions effectively.** Good literary essay writers know that each paragraph must be clearly and strongly linked to the material around it. Think of each paragraph as a response to the one that precedes it. Use transition words and phrases such as *however, similarly, on the contrary, therefore,* and *furthermore* to indicate what kind of response you're making.

---

7. WRITE THE CONCLUSION

Just as you used the introduction to ground your readers in the topic before providing your thesis, you'll use the conclusion to quickly summarize the specifics learned thus far and then hint at the broader implications of your topic. A good conclusion will:

- **Do more than simply restate the thesis.** If your thesis argued that *The Catcher in the Rye* can be read as a Christian allegory, don't simply end your essay by saying, "And that is why *The Catcher in the Rye* can be read as a Christian allegory." If you've constructed your arguments well, this kind of statement will just be redundant.

- **Synthesize the arguments, not summarize them.** Similarly, don't repeat the details of your body paragraphs in your conclusion. The reader has already read your essay, and chances are it's not so long that they've forgotten all your points by now.

- **Revisit the "So what?" question.** In your introduction, you made a case for why your topic and position are important. You should close your essay with the same sort of gesture. What do your readers know now that they didn't know before? How will that knowledge help them better appreciate or understand the work overall?

- **Move from the specific to the general.** Your essay has most likely treated a very specific element of the work—a single character, a small set of images, or a particular passage. In your conclusion, try to show how this narrow discussion has wider implications for the work overall. If your essay on *To Kill a Mockingbird* focused on the character of Boo Radley, for example, you might want to include a bit in your conclusion about how he fits into the novel's larger message about childhood, innocence, or family life.

- **Stay relevant.** Your conclusion should suggest new directions of thought, but it shouldn't be treated as an opportunity to pad your essay with all the extra, interesting ideas you came up with during your brainstorming sessions but couldn't fit into the essay proper. Don't attempt to stuff in unrelated queries or too many abstract thoughts.

- **Avoid making overblown closing statements.** A conclusion should open up your highly specific, focused discussion, but it should do so without drawing a sweeping lesson about life or human nature. Making such observations may be part of the point of reading, but it's almost always a mistake in essays, where these observations tend to sound overly dramatic or simply silly.

A+ ESSAY CHECKLIST

Congratulations! If you've followed all the steps we've outlined above, you should have a solid literary essay to show for all your efforts. What if you've got your sights set on an A+? To write the kind of superlative essay that will be rewarded with a perfect grade, keep the following rubric in mind. These are the qualities that teachers expect to see in a truly A+ essay. How does yours stack up?

- ✓ Demonstrates a thorough understanding of the book
- ✓ Presents an original, compelling argument
- ✓ Thoughtfully analyzes the text's formal elements
- ✓ Uses appropriate and insightful examples
- ✓ Structures ideas in a logical and progressive order
- ✓ Demonstrates a mastery of sentence construction, transitions, grammar, spelling, and word choice

Suggested Essay Topics

1. *How do Jem and Scout change during the course of the novel? How do they remain the same?*

2. *What is Atticus's relationship to the rest of Maycomb? What is his role in the community?*

3. *Discuss the role of family in* To Kill a Mockingbird, *paying close attention to Aunt Alexandra.*

4. *Examine Miss Maudie's relationship to the Finches and to the rest of Maycomb.*

5. *Discuss the author's descriptions of Maycomb. What is the town's role in the novel?*

A+ Student Essay

> What role does Boo Radley play in Scout and Jem's lives
> and in their development?

In *To Kill a Mockingbird,* children live in an inventive world where mysteries abound but little exists to actually cause them harm. Scout and Jem spend much of their time inventing stories about their reclusive neighbor Boo Radley, gleefully scaring themselves before rushing to the secure, calming presence of their father, Atticus. As the novel progresses, however, the imaginary threat that Boo Radley poses pales in comparison to the real dangers Jem and Scout encounter in the adult world. The siblings' recognition of the difference between the two pushes them out of childhood and toward maturity—and as they make that transition, Boo Radley, their childhood bogeyman, helps serve as link between their past and their present.

The games and stories Jem and Scout create around Boo Radley depict him as a source of violence and danger. However, though these inventions seem designed to prove the children's braveness and maturity, they paradoxically prove that Jem, Scout, and their friend Dill fundamentally remain children. Their stories are gruesome, and the thrill of their games—such as touching the side of Boo's house—comes from the danger they imagine they would face if Boo were to catch them. However, the children are able to indulge in wild imaginings and take what they perceive as risky chances only because they feel completely safe in the care of Atticus, who protects them from a dark, dangerous world. The threatening, menacing Boo thus remains firmly entrenched in their childhood worldview, where adults are infallible and all-powerful.

When adult protection breaks down in the novel, Jem and Scout get their first taste of true danger, which is different from the imagined dangers they'd attributed to Boo Radley. The fire at Miss Maudie's, Mrs. Dubose's grisly death, and the violence and unrest that trails in the wake of the Tom Robinson case introduce real misfortune and anxiety into their lives. For the first time, adults are frightened and sad along with the children, and therefore cannot be counted on to provide security or refuge. Boo Radley, once such a threatening presence, now seems like a remnant of a more innocent time. The contrast between then and now seems all the more stark because Boo Radley remains in their lives, a constant reminder of how things had been before.

Faced with real dangers, Jem and Scout must tap into new levels of maturity in order to deal with tragedy, new social challenges, and increased familial expectations. As their relationship with Atticus and the larger adult community changes, their relationship with Boo changes as well. Once just a creepy, mostly abstract figure, Boo begins playing a more active role in the children's lives, first by protecting Scout with a blanket during Miss Maudie's fire and then by protecting Jem and Scout from an attack by Bob Ewell. Boo had been an integral part of Jem and Scout's childhood, and, in the midst of their burgeoning adulthood, he serves as a link between their past and their present. Once an imagined enemy and a source of perceived danger, Boo transforms into a true friend and ally, helping them at crucial moments in their transition from childhood to maturity.

The children's early perspective of "danger" centered on Boo Radley, and only by understanding the contrast between these imagined dangers and the real dangers of the adult world can they pass from childhood into adulthood. But the children's shifting interactions with Boo points to another element of maturity as well: the capacity for empathy. Once simply an eccentric figure in the children's games, Boo ultimately becomes a true human being to them—one who has endured more than his fair share of tragedy and deserves his fair share of honor, respect, and affection.

Glossary of Literary Terms

ANTAGONIST

The entity that acts to frustrate the goals of the *protagonist*. The antagonist is usually another *character* but may also be a non-human force.

ANTIHERO / ANTIHEROINE

A *protagonist* who is not admirable or who challenges notions of what should be considered admirable.

CHARACTER

A person, animal, or any other thing with a personality that appears in a *narrative*.

CLIMAX

The moment of greatest intensity in a text or the major turning point in the *plot*.

CONFLICT

The central struggle that moves the *plot* forward. The conflict can be the *protagonist*'s struggle against fate, nature, society, or another person.

FIRST-PERSON POINT OF VIEW

A literary style in which the *narrator* tells the story from his or her own *point of view* and refers to himself or herself as "I." The narrator may be an active participant in the story or just an observer.

HERO / HEROINE

The principal *character* in a literary work or *narrative*.

IMAGERY

Language that brings to mind sense-impressions, representing things that can be seen, smelled, heard, tasted, or touched.

MOTIF

A recurring idea, structure, contrast, or device that develops or informs the major *themes* of a work of literature.

NARRATIVE

A story.

NARRATOR

The person (sometimes a *character*) who tells a story; the *voice* assumed by the writer. The narrator and the author of the work of literature are not the same person.

PLOT

The arrangement of the events in a story, including the sequence in which they are told, the relative emphasis they are given, and the causal connections between events.

POINT OF VIEW

The *perspective* that a *narrative* takes toward the events it describes.

PROTAGONIST

The main *character* around whom the story revolves.

SETTING

The location of a *narrative* in time and space. Setting creates mood or atmosphere.

SUBPLOT

A secondary *plot* that is of less importance to the overall story but may serve as a point of contrast or comparison to the main plot.

SYMBOL

An object, *character,* figure, or color that is used to represent an abstract idea or concept. Unlike an *emblem,* a symbol may have different meanings in different contexts.

SYNTAX

The way the words in a piece of writing are put together to form lines, phrases, or clauses; the basic structure of a piece of writing.

THEME

A fundamental and universal idea explored in a literary work.

TONE

The author's attitude toward the subject or *characters* of a story or poem or toward the reader.

VOICE

An author's individual way of using language to reflect his or her own personality and attitudes. An author communicates voice through *tone, diction,* and *syntax.*

LITERARY ANALYSIS

A NOTE ON PLAGIARISM

Plagiarism—presenting someone else's work as your own—rears its ugly head in many forms. Many students know that copying text without citing it is unacceptable. But some don't realize that even if you're not quoting directly, but instead are paraphrasing or summarizing, *it is plagiarism* unless you cite the source.

Here are the most common forms of plagiarism:

- Using an author's phrases, sentences, or paragraphs without citing the source
- Paraphrasing an author's ideas without citing the source
- Passing off another student's work as your own

How do you steer clear of plagiarism? You should *always* acknowledge all words and ideas that aren't your own by using quotation marks around verbatim text or citations like footnotes and endnotes to note another writer's ideas. For more information on how to give credit when credit is due, ask your teacher for guidance or visit www.sparknotes.com.

Review & Resources

Quiz

1. What is Scout's real name?

    A. Jean Louise Finch
    B. Louise Marie Finch
    C. Louise Scout Finch
    D. Lee Mae Finch

2. What is the verdict in the Tom Robinson case?

    A. Innocent
    B. Guilty
    C. The jury is hung.
    D. The judge calls a mistrial.

3. Whose house burns down?

    A. Aunt Alexandra's
    B. Atticus's
    C. Mr. Underwood's
    D. Miss Maudie's

4. Who is the editor of the local newspaper?

    A. Mr. Raymond
    B. Atticus
    C. Mr. Underwood
    D. Heck Tate

5. Who insists that Bob Ewell's death is an accident?

    A. Heck Tate
    B. `Atticus
    C. Scout
    D. Boo Radley

6. What is Boo's real name?

    A. Hector
    B. Arthur
    C. Riley
    D. Robert

7. What does Scout first find in the knot-hole?

    A. Bird's nest
    B. Gun
    C. Small bug
    D. Chewing gum

8. What does Dill find in Dolphus Raymond's bottle?

    A. Wine
    B. Whiskey
    C. Coca-Cola
    D. Water

9. Why does Atticus admire Mrs. Dubose?

    A. Because she has courage
    B. Because she is committed to racial equality
    C. Because she is beautiful
    D. Because she is a proud Confederate

10. Who founded Finch's Landing?

    A. Atticus
    B. Simon Finch
    C. Uncle Jack
    D. Jasper Finch

11. How did Miss Caroline learn her educational techniques?

    A. From long experience
    B. From a magazine article
    C. From talking to other teachers
    D. From college courses

12. Who is the president of the United States at the time that the events of the story occur?

    A.   Theodore Roosevelt
    B.   Harry Truman
    C.   Franklin D. Roosevelt
    D.   John F. Kennedy

13. Who tells Jem that it is a sin to kill mockingbirds?

    A.   Atticus
    B.   Miss Maudie and Aunt Alexandra
    C.   Scout
    D.   Dill

14. Where does Dill live during the school year?

    A.   Arkansas
    B.   Mississippi
    C.   Georgia
    D.   Boston

15. On what writer did Harper Lee base Dill?

    A.   Ernest Hemingway
    B.   Mary McCarthy
    C.   Gustave Flaubert
    D.   Truman Capote

16. Who tucks Scout in at the end of the novel?

    A.   Aunt Alexandra
    B.   Boo Radley
    C.   Atticus
    D.   Heck Tate

17. Who beat Mayella Ewell?

    A.   Bob Ewell
    B.   Boo Radley
    C.   Tom Robinson
    D.   Heck Tate

18. Whose actions lead Mr. Cunningham to disperse the lynch mob?

    A. Atticus's
    B. Scout's
    C. Jem's
    D. Mr. Underwood's

19. How old is Jem when the action of the novel starts?

    A. 8
    B. 7
    C. 10
    D. 9

20. What are Jem and Scout shocked to discover about Atticus?

    A. That he can play the fiddle
    B. That he can swim faster than any man in Maycomb
    C. That he is the best shot in Maycomb County
    D. That he is a prize-winning songwriter

21. Who takes the children to the black church?

    A. Calpurnia
    B. Miss Maudie
    C. Helen Robinson
    D. Reverend Sykes

22. Where does Boo leave presents for Scout and Jem?

    A. In a box on his porch
    B. In a hole in an oak tree
    C. In their mailbox
    D. On their windowsills

23. Who mends Jem's pants?

    A. Miss Maudie
    B. Aunt Alexandra
    C. Scout
    D. Boo

24. Who runs away from home?

    A. Scout
    B. Jem
    C. Dill
    D. Francis

25. For what does Uncle Jack reprimand Scout on Christmas Eve?

    A. Cursing
    B. Refusing to play with Francis
    C. Not dressing in a ladylike way
    D. Opening her presents before she was supposed to

ANSWER KEY

1: A; 2: B; 3: D; 4: C; 5: A; 6: B; 7: D; 8: C; 9: A; 10: B; 11: D; 12: C; 13: A; 14: B; 15: D; 16: C; 17: A; 18: B; 19: D; 20: C; 21: A; 22: B; 23: D; 24: C; 25: A

SUGGESTIONS FOR FURTHER READING

BLOOM, HAROLD. *Harper Lee's* TO KILL A MOCKINGBIRD. New York: Chelsea House Publishers, reprint edition 2006.

HASKINS, JAMES. *The Scottsboro Boys*. New York: Henry Holt and Company, 1994.

JOHNSON, CLAUDIA DURST. TO KILL A MOCKINGBIRD: *Threatening Boundaries*. New York: Twayne Publishers, 1994.

O'NEILL, TERRY. *Readings on* TO KILL A MOCKINGBIRD. San Diego, CA: Greenhaven Press, 2000.

POWER, CATHY KELLY. *Thirteen Ways of Looking at a Mockingbird: A Collection of Critical Essays*. Atlanta: Georgia State University Press, 1996.

SHIELDS, CHARLES J. *Mockingbird: A Portrait of Harper Lee*. New York: Henry Holt and Company, 2007.